George Orwell

Battling Big Brother

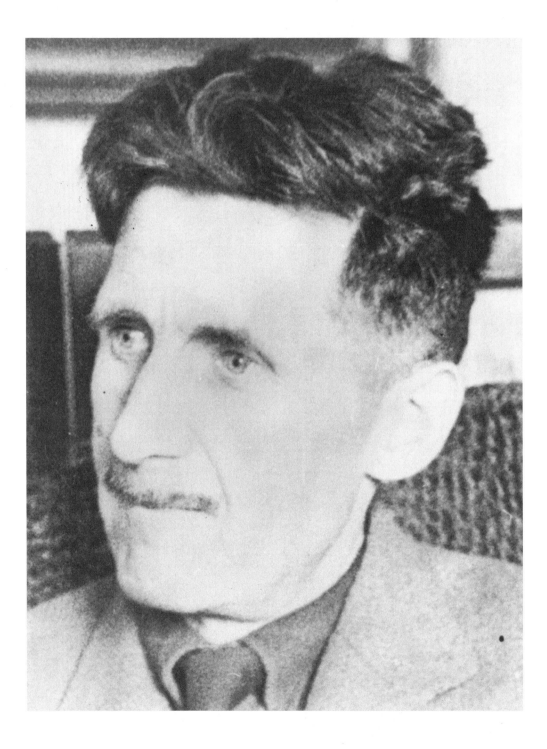

OXFORD
PORTRAITS

George Orwell

Battling Big Brother

Tanya Agathocleous

Oxford University Press

New York • Oxford

OXFORD
UNIVERSITY PRESS

Oxford   New York
Athens   Auckland   Bangkok   Bogotá   Buenos Aires   Calcutta
Cape Town   Chennai   Dar es Salaam   Delhi   Florence   Hong Kong   Istanbul
Karachi   Kuala Lumpur   Madrid   Melbourne   Mexico City   Mumbai
Nairobi   Paris   São Paulo   Singapore   Taipei   Tokyo   Toronto   Warsaw
and associated companies in
Berlin   Ibadan

Design: Greg Wozney
Layout: Alexis Siroc
Picture research: Lisa Kirchner

Library of Congress Cataloging-in-Publication Data
Agathocleous, Tanya, 1970–
George Orwell: Battling Big Brother
p. cm. – (Oxford Portraits)
Includes bibliographical references and index.
Summary: Examines life of George Orwell, the English author of "Animal Farm"
and "1984," and discusses the political and social criticism disclosed in his work.
ISBN 0-19-512185-6 (acid-free paper)
Orwell, George, 1903–1950—Juvenile literature. 2. Authors, English—20th
century—Biography—Juvenile literature. 3. Literature and society—England—
History—20th century—Juvenile literature. [1. Orwell, George, 1903–1950.
2. Authors, English. 3. English literature—History and criticism.] I Title.
II. Oxford Portraits series
PR6029.R8 Z55 2000
828'.91209—dc21
[B]
99-086163

9 8 7 6 5 4 3 2 1

Printed in the United States of America
on acid-free paper

On the cover: George Orwell in 1936.
Frontispiece: Orwell in 1945, the year *Animal Farm* was published.

CONTENTS

Eric (right) spent his school vacations with his close friends the Buddicoms. In her memoir of the summers she spent with Orwell, Jacintha Buddicom wrote, "Out of doors, the games we mostly played were croquet, rounders, and French cricket—because there were not enough of us for anything else."

BEGINNINGS

In 1948, on the tiny, windswept island of Jura off the coast of Scotland, a writer typed away furiously. Occasionally, he was interrupted by a coughing fit and had to stop to spit out blood. On some days he was so weak he typed lying down, the typewriter balanced on his lap. The writer was racing against time. His name was George Orwell, and he was dying of tuberculosis.

The manuscript that was so important to him was finally finished that year, just before his illness overcame him, and he was forced to leave his beloved island to get medical attention. The title of his manuscript was an inversion of the last two numbers of the current year, and a date in the not-too-distant future: *Nineteen Eighty-four.* It was a date he had selected carefully. What might society be like when his son was his age, if the injustices and suffering he had witnessed during World War II continued unchecked? The book that asked that question was a dark, terrifying vision of a world without freedom. As a follow-up to *Animal Farm,* the biting political satire he had published three years earlier, *Nineteen Eighty-four* was an instant success and finally brought him the fame and recognition he had sought for years.

His writing career had always been a struggle. More than 20 publishers in England and America turned down *Animal Farm;* one of the rejections came from the poet T. S. Eliot, then working as an editor in London. It was finally accepted by an editor named Fredric Warburg, who later pointed out that if he had not come along in time, Orwell might have given up and never gone on to write *Nineteen Eighty-four.* "Had that happened," Warburg once said, "the face of English literature in the second quarter of this century would have a measurably different aspect."

Orwell lived to witness only the beginning of his success as a writer. He died at 46, two years after finishing *Nineteen Eighty-four.* His fame spread rapidly after his death and his final novel was hailed as the work of a visionary and profoundly committed political thinker. Today his writing is read in more than 50 languages around the world, and George Orwell has become a legend. Not everyone knows, though, that the life of this renowned author was as extraordinary as his celebrated novels.

He was not born George Orwell. In Bengal, India, on June 25, 1903, Richard Walmesley Blair and Ida Mabel Blair named their newborn son Eric Arthur. Many years later, when his first book, *Down and Out in Paris and London,* was published, Eric Arthur Blair, unsure of the book's merits, adopted the pen name George Orwell (the name "Orwell" was borrowed from one of his favorite English rivers).

His parents were British, of Scottish origin, but their families had for years lived and worked in India, then part of the British Empire. One of Orwell's grandfathers had been a

Ida Mabel Limouzin Blair, Orwell's mother, holds the infant Eric. An artistic and energetic woman who practiced amateur photography and sympathized with the woman suffrage movement, she was described as bohemian and "gypsy-like" in appearance by one of Orwell's classmates.

teak merchant; the other had served in the Indian Army. His father worked for the Indian Civil Service in the Opium Division, overseeing Britain's then-legal opium trade with China. In 1896, at the age of 40, he married Orwell's mother, Ida Limouzin, who was 18 years his junior. In 1907, the Blairs moved back to England so their children could be educated there. Once his family was settled, Richard Blair returned to India alone and continued working there for a number of years. Orwell later said "I barely saw my father before I was eight." He remembered him as a stern, quiet man who often said "Don't." Eric, his mother, and his sister, Marjorie, settled down comfortably in a quaint town named Henley-on-

Thames. Their house was called Ermadale, a name invented by Orwell's mother, using the first letters of her children's names. A second sister, Avril, was born a year later.

Orwell displayed an interest in writing at a remarkably young age. As an adult, he remembered his early aspirations: "I knew that when I grew up I should be a writer." He wryly recalled his first creative efforts: "I wrote my first poem at the age of four or five, my mother taking it down to dictation. I cannot remember anything about it except that it was about a tiger and the tiger had 'chair-like teeth'—a good enough phrase, but I fancy the poem was a plagiarism of Blake's 'Tiger, Tiger.'" Young Eric was a talented student, and in 1911 he won a scholarship to St. Cyprian's, a prestigious boarding school on the southern coast of England. His time there was to be an

Called "superbly unadventurous" by one of his relatives, Richard Walmesley Blair, Orwell's father, tended to observe routines and dress carefully and conservatively.

unpleasant experience that he remembered bitterly for the rest of his life.

St. Cyprian's was a private boys' school and many of its students came from wealthy families: One boy was rumored to be a prince. Writing about the school later in an ironically titled essay, "Such, Such Were the Joys," Orwell remembered feeling mistreated and bullied for being a scholarship boy. On one occasion, a fellow student demanded to know how much money his father made and sneered at him when he named the figure. Boys who were not clearly rich, Orwell wrote later, were questioned closely to determine their social status:

> How much a year has your pater got? What part of London do you live in? Is that Knightsbridge or Kensington? How many bathrooms has your house got? How many servants do your people keep? Have you got a butler? Well, then, have you got a cook? Where do you get your clothes made? How many shows did you go to in the hols? How much money did you bring back with you? etc. etc.

The rich boys were also treated better by the grown-ups, Orwell felt, whereas the less privileged were expected to work extra hard to prove their worth. Scholarship students were considered an investment—they had the potential to win further scholarships to famous schools like Eton, bringing prestige to St. Cyprian's and its owners.

As well as an atmosphere of snobbery, the boys at St. Cyprian's faced regular canings, hard mattresses, and lumpy, often inedible porridge. The school's owners, Mr. and Mrs. Vaughan Wilkes, inspired terror in the children by punishing them at every turn and deliberately choosing favorites, who were then resented by the other students. Orwell summed up his school experience as an "overcrowded, underfed, unwashed life." He suffered from a chronic cough, later diagnosed as tuberculosis, a serious lung condition that would eventually lead to his death. But his wheezing during sports prompted his teachers to make him run even faster to "cure" it. The school's emphasis on building character and its disdain for weakness fueled Orwell's lifelong indignation at abuses of power in any form. He saw at St. Cyprian's a "pattern of school life—a continuous triumph of the strong over the weak....Life was hierarchical and whatever happened was right."

Nonetheless, there were some good times to be had. Eric loved the cricket games the students played, and reported on them regularly to his mother, also inquiring diligently after the family dog and guinea pig. A sympathetic teacher, Robert Sillar, befriended him and encouraged the boy's passion for nature by helping him find butterflies and caterpillars to raise. Meanwhile, his interest in writing continued unabated. He read avidly whenever he could, enjoying the novels of William Makepeace Thackeray, Rudyard Kipling, and H. G. Wells. He and his friend Cyril Connolly exchanged and critiqued each other's poems. These activities, it turned out, were practice for important literary contributions to come. Connolly later became a well-known editor who would publish Orwell's essays in his magazine, *Horizon*. Separated after school, they met again when Connolly reviewed his old friend's first novel; Connolly later introduced Orwell to the latter's second wife, Sonia Brownell. Of his time with Orwell at St. Cyprian's, Connolly wrote: "I was a stage rebel, Orwell a true one. Tall, pale, with his flaccid cheeks, and a matter-of-fact, supercilious voice, he was one of those boys who seem born old.... Orwell proved to me that there existed an alternative to Character, Intelligence."

Cyril Connolly, Orwell's good friend and fellow student at St. Cyprian's, shared his interest in literature in school and later became an editor of his work. Fellow student Cecil Beaton, who would become a famous photographer, took this picture of Connolly.

When Eric was 11, World War I broke out, and everyday life was dramatically transformed. School activities were adjusted to fit the times. The boys were taken to hospitals to comfort wounded soldiers, and the names of former students killed in action were announced regularly. A wave of patriotic fervor and anti–German sentiment swept the nation. Eric, caught up in the spirit of the times, wrote a poem that was published in a local newspaper, the *Henley and South Oxfordshire Standard*. It ended with a strident call to duty:

> Awake! Oh you young men of England,
> For if when your country's in need,
> You do not enlist by the thousand,
> You truly are cowards indeed.

After its publication, the principal proudly read the poem to the entire school. For a brief time, Eric was a hero.

But for most of his school years, Eric felt isolated and lonely. His creativity served as a consolation. In a essay titled "Why I Write," Orwell described how, as a child, he continually made up stories in which he had the starring role:

> For minutes at a time this kind of thing would be running through my head: "He pushed the door open and entered the room. A yellow beam of sunlight, filtering through the muslin curtains, slanted on to the table, where a matchbox, half-open, lay beside the inkpot. With his right hand in his pocket he moved across to the window. Down in the street a tortoiseshell cat was chasing a dead leaf, etc., etc."

Going home during breaks was a welcome change from school, presenting Eric with ample time to read and indulge his imagination. Although his childhood friend Jacintha Buddicom remembered him as a loner who never brought friends home during vacation, he was close to her and her brothers. When she first met Eric he was standing on his head. The world, he told her, looked more interesting from that perspective. They became fast friends and, during the summer months on break from school, were virtually inseparable.

Jacintha and Eric shared a love for literature, and he encouraged her to read, bringing her books and borrowing hers. He was particularly fond of ghost stories, and once presented Jacintha with a copy of *Dracula,* together with a crucifix and clove of garlic carefully wrapped in tissue paper, to ward off vampires. In order to write, Eric advised Jacintha, one must read constantly. "Of course, Eric was always going to write," Jacintha recalled in her memoirs, "not merely as an author, always a FAMOUS AUTHOR, in capitals."

At the age of 13, Eric sat through a series of scholarship exams, including an exhausting two-and-a-half day marathon exam, for admittance to Eton. It was typical of St. Cyprian's emphasis on rote learning that everything he had studied over the last five years would be tested on only these few tense days. Orwell pointed out the folly of this system of learning in "Such, Such Were the Joys":

> I recall positive orgies of dates, with the keener boys leaping up and down in their places in their eagerness to shout out the right answers, and at the same time not feeling the faintest interest in the meaning of the mysterious events they were naming.
>
> "1587?"
> "Massacre of St. Bartholomew!"
> "1707?"
> "Death of Aurangzeeb!"
> "1713?"
> "Treaty of Utrecht!"

Despite his later disdain for the exams, Eric did reasonably well on them. He was immediately accepted by a well-known military school, Wellington College, but had to wait to hear if a spot was open for him at Eton. In the meantime, he now had an alternative to the hated St. Cyprian's. One week before Christmas, 1916, he left the school forever, thrilled at his escape: "How happy I was, that winter morning, as the train bore me away with the gleaming new silk tie (dark green, pale blue and black, if I remember rightly) round my neck! The world was opening before me, just a little, like a grey sky which exhibits a narrow crack of blue." Wellington, however, did not prove to be any more agreeable than St. Cyprian's. Fortunately, he was not there for very long. After nine weeks, he learned that he had won a prestigious King's scholarship to Eton.

Eton was a snobbish place, too. Orwell later described it as "the most costly and snobbish of the English Public Schools." ("Public school," paradoxically, is the British term for a private boarding school for high-school-age students. Those who could afford them generally considered such schools superior to state schools.) It was certainly the most esteemed public school for, as popular lore had it, England's battles were won "on the playing fields of Eton." Those who attended it were expected to go on to Oxford and Cambridge and eventually become leaders of British society.

The boys there divided themselves up into Oppidans and Collegers. "College" was a section of Eton made up of King's Scholars like Eric, who lived in the school's oldest buildings. The Oppidans made up the rest of Eton and were generally wealthier than the Collegers; their name originated from the Latin word "oppidanus," meaning "belonging to a town" because they had originally boarded with private families in town. Oppidans tended to sneer at Collegers for being middle-class and teachers' pets to boot, while the Collegers taunted them back, accusing them of being rich but brainless. Just as at St. Cyprian's, the boys were often beaten for minor offenses.

Despite all this, Eric liked Eton better than his former school. He was older and more self-assured now, and there were some perks to being a teenager: "At Eton you had a room to yourself—a room which might even have a fire in it....The privacy of it, the grown-upness!" Though he did not excel academically at Eton, Eric did continue to write industriously, and involved himself in Eton's literary world. He produced several satirical poems and short stories for various school publications, and served as business manager for Eton's magazine, *Election Times.* For another magazine, *College Days,* he served as editor, promoting its success by selling copies at the annual Eton-versus-Harrow cricket match.

Eric was becoming especially fascinated by the nature of language. "When I was about sixteen," he was to write later, "I suddenly discovered the joy of mere words, i.e. the sounds and associations of words." One year, he briefly

Though Orwell did not have special affection for Eton, it was a relief from St. Cyprian's, and he later said that it had "a tolerant and civilized atmosphere which gives each boy a fair chance of developing his own individuality."

studied French with Aldous Huxley, who was substitute teaching at Eton for a year. Though his contact with Huxley was brief, the teacher's command of language and careful use of words was an inspiration to Eric. Little did he know that Huxley would go on to write *Brave New World*, a celebrated novel that would draw constant comparison to *Nineteen Eighty-four*. Huxley himself was later so impressed by *Nineteen Eighty-four* that he wrote Orwell a warm letter of praise.

While Eric was comfortably isolated at Eton, World War I was still raging. His family moved to London, and his mother and elder sister, Marjorie, took on full-time jobs as part of the war effort. His father, at the age of 60, had volunteered for the army and was fighting as a second lieutenant. Later, Orwell described the guilt he and his contemporaries felt because they had not been old enough to serve in the war: "My particular generation, those who had been 'just too young,' became conscious of the vastness of the experience they had missed. You felt yourself a little less than a man, because you had missed it."

Because Eric had not performed well academically at Eton, the path pursued by most of its graduates—going to college at Oxford or Cambridge—was not a given for him. Instead, Eric made a decision he would later regret. Partly from the need to prove his worth by taking on grown-up responsibility, and partly to follow in his family's career path, he decided not to apply to college after graduating from Eton. Instead, in 1922, he boarded the *SS Herefordshire* and sailed to Rangoon, Burma, to begin a career as a policeman in the Indian Imperial Police.

Burma, a Southeast Asian nation now called Myanmar, was one of the regions administered by the Indian police force. The British Empire at this time was an enormous, sprawling dominion that covered large parts of the globe. Begun as a network of British trading posts in the 17th century, the Empire was consolidated under Queen

Victoria in the late 19th century when trading posts became territories controlled by British administrators. India was one of the largest territories held by Britain, and it was known as "the jewel in the crown."

One of Eric's grandmothers and an aunt lived in Burma, which may have been why he chose this post. Regardless of what initially motivated him to work in Burma in the service of the Empire, he soon came to regret his decision. He later described his stint as policeman as "five boring years within the sound of bugles," but boredom was actually the least of his problems.

The years Eric Blair served as an imperial policeman saw the worst tensions between Britain and Burma since the start of British occupation. The Burmese were beginning to demand independence. Instead of the idyllic, exotic life Blair expected to find in the colonies, judging from the descriptions of writers like Kipling, he found himself in a world where injustice and resentment were the order of the day. Even before he got off the ship in Burma, he witnessed a white police officer kicking a Burmese servant who was struggling under the load of a large piece of luggage on the pier.

As an imperial policeman, Blair's job was to maintain order, which often meant arresting Burmese natives and having them beaten. Occasionally, he was even required to supervise hangings. Not only did he feel ambivalent about being in a country where he was not wanted, but he also loathed these cruel duties. Later on, he would state, "I hated the imperialism I was serving with a bitterness which I probably cannot make clear." As a child, Blair had often felt tyrannized and powerless; as an agent of the British Empire, he had come to know what it was to wield absolute power, and he found that experience equally damaging. His essay "Shooting an Elephant" is based on a real-life incident from his time in Burma, and explores the effect of oppression on the oppressor. The incident occurs when an English policeman is called upon to shoot an elephant that has run amok through a marketplace and killed a local worker. Although he does not want to kill the animal, he feels obliged to do so because a crowd of Burmese has gathered, expecting him to demonstrate his authority:

> I perceived in this moment that when the white man turns tyrant it is his own freedom that he destroys....For it is the condition of his rule that he shall spend his life in trying to impress the 'natives,' and so in every crisis he has got to do what the 'natives' expect of him. He wears a mask, and his face grows to fit it. I had got to shoot the elephant. I had committed myself to doing it when I sent for the rifle.

The policeman eventually shoots the elephant, but does a bad job of it and the elephant dies a horrible death. Grimly, the policeman admits to himself, "I had done it solely to avoid looking a fool."

This sentiment seems to sum up Blair's feelings about his time in Burma. Serving the Empire was a hypocritical endeavor, he decided, and he refused to support the notion that imperialism was about bringing progress to other countries. Earlier writers like Kipling had thought of imperialism as "the White Man's Burden," meaning that it was the duty of Europeans to bring order and Christianity to non-Christian countries. In Orwell's novel *Burmese Days*, loosely based on his experience in Burma, his main character, Flory, dismisses "the slimy white man's burden humbug." Bitterly, Flory asks his friend: "How can you make out that we are in this country for any purpose except to steal? It's so simple. The official holds the Burman down while the business man goes through his pockets."

Burmese Days is a novel that Orwell later dismissed as being long-winded and full of "purple prose," but it reveals the complexity of his impressions of Burma. The book stresses the importance for the British of the imperial Club: the enclave where officers drink heavily to pass the time,

During his time in Burma, Orwell felt hated by all around him and, according to the writer Maung Htin Aung, identified with the outcast status of a rogue elephant.

gossip aimlessly, and talk about the inferiority of the Indians. The adage of most of the British is, "We white men must hang together," but Flory, an imperial policeman by trade, is repelled by his fellow colonials. He has come to hate the attitude of those around him—"What was at the center of his thoughts now, and what poisoned everything, was the ever bitterer hatred of the atmosphere of imperialism in which he lived." Furthermore, unlike the others, Flory enjoys the company of the Burmese and appreciates their culture. As a colonial, though, he is never

Blair stands third from left in the back row at the Police Training School in Mandalay, Burma, 1923. The cruelty and injustice involved in his policeman's duties led him later to write: "I never went into a jail without feeling that my place was on the other side of the bars."

completely accepted by them. Haunted by loneliness, Flory is not courageous enough to dismiss the British, or to leave their ranks, and when an attractive young British woman, Elizabeth, arrives on the scene, Flory is smitten and tries harder than ever to fit in at the Club.

His budding romance with Elizabeth is cut short, though, when Elizabeth, an unimaginative soul, decides that Flory is "unmanly" because he likes poetry and Burmese culture. She becomes more interested in Verrall, a callous, muscular polo player who lures her away from Flory for his own amusement. Meanwhile, Ma Hla May, Flory's Burmese former mistress, is scheming to win him back from his new love interest. One ill-fated morning, she bursts into church and reveals that Flory has had an affair with her, a fact that openly disgusts the racist British. Disgraced, and with Elizabeth lost to him forever, Flory has to face the fact of his complete isolation in Burma. Hopelessness overcomes him, and he commits suicide.

Burmese Days displayed Blair's refusal to shrink from the truth about the destructive nature of illegitimate power. It portrayed both the dishonesty of Burmese officials and the racist attitudes held by many British imperialists. One incident in the book, in which a bigot named Ellis hits a Burmese boy with a stick, was based on an occasion when Blair himself had performed a similar action. Unlike many other colonials, Blair was willing to confront his demons. He was also willing, like Flory, to learn the culture around him and made a successful effort to learn the Burmese language. Over time, he grew increasingly sympathetic to the native struggle. He would later argue in newspaper articles that Burmese demands for self-government should be taken seriously.

Blair worked for the Imperial Police for five years before abruptly resigning from the service in 1927, while on leave in England. Not only could he no longer endure his job as policeman, but he also felt he had lost sight of his lifelong dream of becoming a writer. His recent experiences had been daunting, but they contributed to a renewed sense of purpose. He began a new life in England, determined to listen to his conscience and to make a living from his craft.

By experimenting with being "down and out" like this Parisian, Orwell gained a distinctly unromantic view on the life of the homeless poor he befriended: "You thought it would be terrible: it is merely squalid and boring."

HOW THE POOR LIVE

Blair returned from Burma a changed man, his sister Avril later noted. He sported a military-style, stick-thin mustache and had developed slovenly habits, for he had grown used to Burmese servants cleaning up after him. His parents had been proud when Eric had left for India, for they had been counting on their only son to carry on the family tradition of serving the British government. Now, much to his parents' distress, he informed them that he would not be returning to Burma, and worse, that he was determined to make a living as a writer. Sonia Pitt, a family friend, recalled that this announcement "filled us all with horror." Not only was the occupation of writer considered an impractical career goal, but no one—not even A. S. F. Gow, his tutor from Eton who now served as one of his literary mentors— believed he had the talent or persistence it required.

Unfazed by the lack of enthusiasm he encountered, Blair was exhilarated at his newfound freedom. He had escaped the oppressive system he despised and could now dictate his own life. He began writing profusely, initially with more enthusiasm than skill. Sonia Pitt, a writer herself, and therefore a natural ally for Blair, later said that she and her friends could not help but laugh at the awkward poems he earnestly presented her with. His clumsy efforts, she said, were reminiscent of a "cow with a musket." Despite the fact that she was unimpressed by Blair's first attempts at authorship, Sonia gave him sound advice. She suggested he try prose instead of poetry and reminded him of the age-old principle of good writing: Write what you know.

In order to write about what he knew, and more important, what he cared about, Blair realized he still had a lot to learn. Boarding school and Burma had taught him that he hated any system in which power was used by the strong to dominate and intimidate the weak. He realized that he cared deeply about the suffering of others and decided to try to see things from the perspective of those who suffered the most in his society: the homeless poor. So began the first of his sojourns in London's East End. Following the example of the American writer Jack London, who had once written about the slums of London himself, Blair began to embark on expeditions dressed in tramp's clothing. If he looked like he had been "down and out" for a while, he reasoned, other tramps would not treat him as if he were different from themselves, and he would get a more realistic picture of what poverty was like. Clothes, he found, were a crucial part of one's identity. As soon as he put on his "uniform" of baggy, ill-fitting clothes, he was transformed beyond recognition. This was driven home to him one day when he was approached by a bedraggled tramp and it took him at least a few seconds to realize that it was, in fact, his own reflection in a shop window.

In 1928, Blair decided to continue his pursuit of new experiences in Paris, a mecca for writers of the period. Gertrude Stein was there, surrounded by fashionable figures of the day, as was James Joyce, who Blair once thought he glimpsed walking down the street. In his essay "Inside the Whale," he recounted the intoxicating atmosphere of the city: "Paris was invaded by such a swarm of artists, writers, students, dilettanti, sight-seers, debauchees and plain idlers as the world has probably never seen."

When he first arrived in Paris, he stayed briefly with his aunt, Nellie Limouzin Adam, but then moved to a tenement hotel in the Latin Quarter of the Left Bank. At the time, the Left Bank was highly popular with artists and those with little money. Blair, for the moment, qualified as both. His address was 6, Rue du Pot-de-Fer, which he would later disguise as "Rue du Coq d'Or" in *Down and Out in Paris and London,* the book that served as a testament to his days of poverty. The street, by his account, was a place of

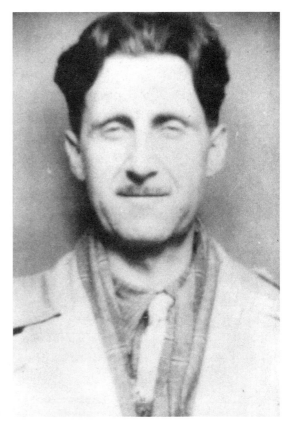

During the late 1920s, Blair went back and forth between the life of a writer and that of a tramp, changing into different outfits for each of the roles. Here he is in tramp costume.

sharp sounds and smells: "Quarrels, and the desolate cries of street hawkers, and the shouts of children chasing orange-peel over the cobbles, and at night loud singing and the sour reek of the refuse-carts, made up the atmosphere of the street."

Early on during his stay in Paris, Blair, never in perfect health even at the best of times, came down with a bad case of pneumonia. He was forced to stay at the Hôpital Cochin, a hospital for nonpaying patients. There he had one of the more traumatic experiences of his "down-and-out" days, which he recorded years later in a famous essay "How the Poor Die." The inexperienced medical students who were allowed to practice on the poor subjected them to grim and no doubt harmful procedures, such as "cupping." This involved creating a vacuum within a glass,

25

placing it on the patient's back to create a blood blister, and then draining the blister to produce a spoonful of blood. The atmosphere at the hospital was equally grim, and reminded Blair of what he had read about the "reeking, pain-filled" conditions of 19th-century hospitals.

Blair was willing to endure suffering, however, in the name of experience and becoming a writer. He wrote continually while in Paris, churning out works of fiction at an extraordinarily fast pace. These writings were seemingly no better than the poems he had shown Sonia, however, for every publisher to whom they were sent rejected them. His journalistic efforts were more successful, fortunately. He sold his first article—on censorship in England—to a reputable French newspaper called *Monde*. He eventually managed to place pieces in English newspapers as well.

Yet he was hardly successful enough to support himself solely by writing. Early on, he managed to eke out a living on his savings from Burma, but inevitably this pool of money ran out, leaving him virtually penniless. Instead of approaching his aunt for support or writing to his family, Blair consciously chose to live a life of poverty. In this, he seems to have been motivated by a variety of factors. He may have felt that a bohemian lifestyle of poverty lent authenticity to his goal of becoming a writer. The bohemians of the Left Bank tended to be artists and writers who were not always poor by birth but chose to live simply in order to show that they cared more about artistic ideals than possessions. But Blair also hinted, in his first nonfiction book, *The Road to Wigan Pier*, that his desire to be poor stemmed from feelings of guilt toward those less privileged than himself. He was ashamed not only of being relatively well off but also of his recent work as an imperial policeman in Burma.

Blair also needed to confront his worst fears about poverty. At school, after being teased for being on scholarship, he had become very conscious and fearful of what it would mean to be truly poor. In *Down and Out in Paris and London,* he wrote of the relief that came from facing these fears at last: "You have talked so often of going to the dogs—and well, here are the dogs, and you have reached them, and you can stand it. It takes off a lot of anxiety." Most important, though, Blair was willing to become one of the poor because he wanted to draw attention to their plight through his writing. He firmly believed that if poverty was to be properly understood, it had to be experienced firsthand.

In the fall of 1929, Blair's family and friends lost touch with him entirely. He temporarily severed all ties to the society he had known, and went incognito among the ranks of the poor. What we know of his life at this time, then, is what he describes of it in *Down and Out in Paris and London.* Although the book was not advertised as autobiography, Blair claimed that it was based almost entirely on experience, and that he had merely rearranged the order of events.

Clearly, one of the worst aspects of being poor was the constant hunger, for he recorded the sensation vividly in his book. He often lived for days on bread and tea alone, and once went without food for two-and-a-half days. Hunger, Blair came to realize, can reduce a human being to nothing more than "a belly with a few accessory organs." Another distressing aspect of his new lifestyle was the number of insects with which he had to contend: "Near the ceiling long lines of bugs marched all day like columns of soldiers, and at night came down ravenously hungry, so that one had to get up every few hours and kill them...." By the end of his days in Paris, he finally learned that the trick to keeping them out of his bed was to shake pepper thickly over the bedclothes: "It made me sneeze, but the bugs all hated it."

Although times were hard, Blair was not entirely friendless. He became close to an excitable Russian refugee, featured as "Boris" in *Down and Out in Paris and London.* Blair and Boris soon became co-conspirators in search of jobs and money. Together they pawned their possessions until there was nothing left in their rooms, and went from hotel to hotel looking for jobs in the kitchen. Boris vacillated between moods of extreme optimism, insisting that they would soon be feasting like kings, and moments of complete despair. His despair was not entirely unwarranted; often the two came home jobless and hungry, and passed the time by fantasizing about the food they would devour once they were rich and famous.

Once, desperate to follow up any lead, they approached an underground communist group, which offered Blair a job as a writer of propaganda. He and Boris were sworn to secrecy, asked to leave money for membership dues, and told to return later, carrying a pile of clothes so it would look as though they were there to use the laundry in the building. When they came back, optimistically sporting a bundle of wash, they found that the group had disappeared, taking the money with them. Blair was impressed at how elaborately they had been swindled: "They were clever fellows, and played their part admirably. Their office looked exactly as a secret Communist office should look, and as for that touch about bringing a parcel of washing, it was genius."

Eventually, the two men found themselves jobs in a run-down Paris hotel. Blair was a dishwasher, and he found the work grueling and tedious. The sweltering heat of the kitchen had the staff dripping with sweat, and they were often reduced to sucking on chunks of ice to cool off. Blair was fascinated by the fact that the hotel employees were divided into a caste system as oppressive as that he had observed in boarding school, and then again as a colonial officer. Here, as in school, he was at the bottom of the ranks, and had to contend with a constant stream of verbal abuse from those above him.

After a few months, Blair tired of his life in Paris. He accepted money from a friend for his voyage back across the English Channel, and returned to his parents' home in Southwold, England. Armed with his new experiences, he began again to work full-time at becoming a writer. He began to write a book tentatively titled *A Scullion's Diary,* which later became part of *Down and Out in Paris and London.* However, the publishers he initially approached with it turned him down. Dejected, but still determined, Blair resumed his tramping expeditions around London, ever on the lookout for new experiences to add to his repertoire.

Using the houses of friends such as Sonia Pitt as "drops," where he could change clothes and record his experiences, Blair would disappear for days at a time. His experience living as a tramp entailed even more hardship than his days of poverty in Paris. Tramps were homeless people (mainly men) with little or no source of income, who were forced to travel the country in search of places to sleep and seasonal work, like picking hops (hops are a type of plant used in the brewing of beer and malt liquor). As a tramp, Blair frequently slept on park benches and in ditches and bathed in public fountains and country streams. In the homeless shelters where he sometimes stayed overnight—known as "spikes" in the tramps' slang—conditions were not much better. He often ended up sleeping on the floor, curled up against the hot-water pipes for warmth. But he also met many interesting people, whose eccentric traits he used as material to create characters for his book. There was "Paddy," the Irish tramp who showed him the ins and outs of life on the road, and "Bozo," the sidewalk artist who made his living creating instant art on the sidewalk.

Blair never completely identified with the poor—his genteel upbringing made it difficult for him to get used to the boredom and hardship of the tramp's lifestyle. But he sympathized with their plight, and in *Down and Out,* attacked commonplace middle-class beliefs about the homeless: "People have been brought up to believe in the tramp-monster, and so they prefer to think that there must be some more or less villainous motive for tramping." Tramps did not tramp with evil motives, he explained, but because they were allowed to stay at the spikes for only one night at a time. Thus they were forced to travel aimlessly around the country, moving from one shelter to another simply to keep a roof over their heads. Orwell did not just attack the system that produced the tramps; he also proposed a solution, suggesting that each shelter become a communal farm where the tramps could work to support themselves.

In 1932, still failing to make a living as a writer, Blair finally decided to seek alternative employment. He had recently had the opportunity to gain some teaching expertise. While staying in Southwold, he had tutored the three young sons of a family named Peters during their summer vacation. One of them, Richard Peters, was later interviewed as an adult, and remembered Blair as a tall, spindly man who had "captivated us completely within five minutes." With the knowledge that he had the ability to relate well to children, Orwell sought employment as a teacher, and eventually landed a job at a small private school called The Hawthorns. He got along well with the boys there, but he found the work tiring and was disturbed by how badly the school was run by its proprietor.

Luckily for Blair, events were transpiring that would eventually give him a way out. When he had finally given up trying to publish the story of his down-and-out days, he had left the manuscript with one of the friends he stayed with while tramping, Mabel Fierz. Fierz was an eccentric, energetic woman whom he had met on the beach one day at Southwold. Passionate about ideas, Fierz surrounded herself with writers and thinkers and encouraged them in their work. She was enthusiastic about Blair's writing from the start, and was one of the few people who were thoroughly convinced he had a gift for it.

It was perhaps for this reason that Blair eventually instructed her to throw away the manuscript he had left at her house—he may have guessed that she would not have the heart to do it and secretly wanted her not to. Far from disposing of the manuscript, in fact, Fierz took it to an agent named Leonard Moore, and pestered him into reading it. Seeing its potential, Moore gave it to Victor Gollancz, publisher of the Left Book Club—a group particularly interested in political writing and the plight of the working class. Gollancz agreed to publish it, provided Blair cut out some of the swearwords and change the names of certain people and places. He was afraid of being sued for the often-unflattering representations that Blair had created.

Blair, meanwhile, had convinced himself that the book was no good, owing to its initial rejection, and insisted that it be published under a pseudonym. He offered the publisher four choices of pen names—P. S. Burton, a name he had used in his tramping days, and three others he made up for the occasion, Kenneth Miles, George Orwell, and H. Lewis Allways. Gollancz had come up with only "X" as a possible pseudonym for Blair. Not surprisingly, perhaps, he decided he liked George Orwell better, and so an author was born. In 1933, *Down and Out in Paris and London* was published. It received good reviews, and Eric Blair became George Orwell to the public, though he kept his birth name for those who already knew him.

The book was not only a commercial but also a critical success. It sold well and was praised by leading writers of the day, such as J. B. Priestley and Henry Miller. Priestley was a British playwright, novelist, and essayist, known for his interest in social issues; Miller was an American author, eventually to become notorious for his frank writing about sex. Their tribute meant a lot to Orwell. His book had caused him much heartache—he later told a friend that he had retyped the entire manuscript five times—but his hard work was finally beginning to pay off. With a first book under his belt, Orwell returned to his writing with renewed energy. In the years that followed, he wrote three novels in quick succession.

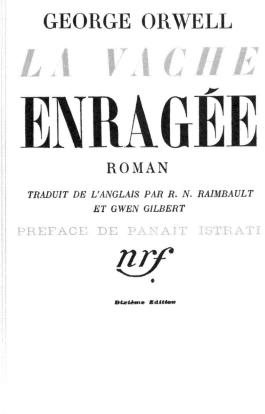

GEORGE ORWELL

LA VACHE

ENRAGÉE

ROMAN

*TRADUIT DE L'ANGLAIS PAR R. N. RAIMBAULT
ET GWEN GILBERT*

PREFACE DE PANAÏT ISTRATI

nrf

Dixième Edition

GALLIMARD

For this 1935 French version of Down and Out in Paris and London, *the title has been changed to* The Angry Cow, *probably a reference to Orwell's frequently enraged Parisian landlady, who is called a cow by an annoyed tenant in the book.*

Burmese Days, published in 1934, came out initially in New York rather than London, as his publisher was worried that Orwell's harsh critique of the Empire would offend the British public. His next two novels, *A Clergyman's Daughter* and *Keep the Aspidistra Flying,* were published in London in 1935 and 1936 respectively. Both drew on his recent experiences, featuring middle-class characters brushing up against poverty.

The inspiration for *A Clergyman's Daughter* appears to have come from Orwell's tramping days, when he once noticed a clergyman and his daughter staring at him in his tramp attire. In the novel, he imagines what their lives might be like, just as they might have been wondering the same about him. Dorothy Hare, the title character, undergoes a loss of faith in the Anglican religion preached by her father. She searches for other ways to provide her life with meaning, but marriage—one of the only ways she can support herself without the help of her father—seems to her a poor alternative. The solution, she eventually decides, is to carry on as if she still believed in the religion that had previously dictated her life and daily responsibilities. She continues, therefore, to live the dutiful, dull existence that we see her rebel against at the beginning of the novel. The novel makes the point that "faith and no faith are very much the same provided that one is doing what is customary, useful and acceptable." It also shows, through Dorothy's return to a life of service, how people often participate in their own oppression—a topic that was to recur frequently in Orwell's writing.

Keep the Aspidistra Flying can also be seen as a novel about a failed revolt. Aspidistra, a houseplant popular in "respectable" middle-class homes, is a symbol of everything the novel's protagonist Gordon Comstock wishes to rebel against. Temporarily successful as an advertising copywriter, Comstock becomes sick of serving "the money god" and decides to live a life of poverty in protest. When his girlfriend, Rosemary, becomes pregnant, however, he realizes that he must return—like Dorothy, the clergyman's daughter—to a life of duty and resumes his advertising job in order to support his family. Pessimistic about the money-driven values of the modern world, the novel was also prophetic about where these values may lead. Comstock, in his morose musings on the "money god," imagines planes darkening the city sky and showering it with bombs—a scenario that Orwell would in fact witness a few years later when World War II broke out.

Orwell was not overly fond of any of these novels once he had finished them, and later referred to them disparagingly in letters to friends, with comments such as: "My novel about Burma made me spew when I saw it in print." Nonetheless, each novel earned its share of critical attention and helped to establish his reputation as an up-and-coming writer.

In 1934, Orwell had left his teaching job to focus on writing, and taken up residence in London, where he was able to supplement his meager writing income with a job as an assistant in a bookshop. At the same time, he worked on building up his literary credentials by writing poetry and book reviews for a magazine called the *Adelphi*. Hampstead, where the bookshop was located, was known as one of London's artistic neighborhoods, and living there gave

Orwell the opportunity to meet others who shared his interest in literature and politics. In 1935, he met an intriguing woman named Eileen O'Shaughnessy at a party, and reportedly told his landlady that she was exactly the kind of person he wanted to marry.

O'Shaughnessy had studied English at Oxford, and earned a master's degree in psychology at University College, London. Intelligent, independent, and unperturbed by Orwell's eccentric lifestyle, she was well suited to him. He nearly proposed a few weeks after their initial meeting, but instead broke down and confessed that he was ashamed to marry her without the proper means to support her. His wife-to-be, apparently, was not concerned about his poverty, for they were married soon afterwards. The couple escaped from the city to a dilapidated house known as The Stores, in the small village of Wallington, in Hertfordshire, about 35 miles north of London. There, they revitalized the old grocery store that had once been part of the house (hence its name) and kept a garden where they planted apple and plum trees and grew vegetables.

Orwell could now afford to live a more sedate life. Just before he was married, he received an interesting and lucrative assignment from his editor, Victor Gollancz. Sensing that Orwell's recent experience of being "down and out" made him a perfect candidate for the job, Gollancz commissioned him to write about the conditions of miners in the north of England for the Left Book Club. He offered him 500 pounds, then a large sum of money, to undertake the venture.

On January 31, 1936, Orwell headed north on foot, sleeping in youth hostels along the way. Five days later he arrived in the town he was to immortalize in his documentary-style book *The Road to Wigan Pier.* The title of the book referred to a decrepit old jetty that had been named Wigan Pier as a joke; the jetty no longer existed but the joke had stuck and its name lived on. Wigan was a bleak

town. The New York stock
market crash of 1929, followed by
the Great Depression, had left
England in a state of severe economic decline. One out of every
four workers was unemployed,
and a high percentage of those
who were employed were under-
paid. Wigan had been particularly
hard hit, and when Orwell
arrived the town was filled with
unemployed miners.

He arranged to stay as a
boarder with a mining family in a
house that doubled as a tripe shop.
On top of the unpleasantness of
the tripe—edible tissue from the
stomachs of cows which attracted
flies—Orwell found his living situation disgusting. His landlady wiped her mouth on blankets and pieces of newspaper,
then left the pieces crumpled up on the floor. One day he
came to breakfast to find a full chamber pot under the table,
and decided to take up residence elsewhere.

Soon after being introduced to Eileen O'Shaughnessy at a party, Orwell wrote, "She is the nicest person I have met for a long time." In 1936, she became his first wife.

Though his landlady's manners were not representative
of the people in Wigan, Orwell was continually aware of
a cultural difference between himself and the working-
class people he encountered in the North. In *The Road
to Wigan Pier,* he called it "that accursed itch of class
difference, like the pea under the princess's mattress." The
reference Orwell uses is to a popular fairy-tale in which a
princess's aristocratic identity is confirmed by the fact that
her sensitive skin can feel a pea even through the thick
layers of a mattress. Like the princess, Orwell felt that his
class position was something from which he could not
escape. Though he had been accepted by the urban poor
he had encountered in Paris and London, he now found

himself an outsider: "Though I was among them and I hope and trust they did not find me a nuisance, I was not one of them and they knew it better than I." For one thing, he was no longer wearing a disguise, and was open about the fact that he was a reporter. Joe Kennan, an electrician who escorted Orwell around the mining town, found the writer aloof, and later said in an interview that Orwell "never showed any appreciation of hospitality, or anything like that. He was kind of up in the air and a snob in some ways, and was trying to come down to earth and find what things was really like."

Though he may have come across as a middle-class snob at times, Orwell was genuinely horrified by the conditions the miners faced, and blamed the harshness of their lives on the dehumanizing aspects of their work. His description of his experience of the mines in *The Road to Wigan Pier* brought out the full horror of the miners' ordeal:

> You have not only got to bend double, you have also to keep your head up all the while so as to see the beams and girders and dodge them when they come. You have, therefore, a constant crick in the neck, but this is nothing to the pain in your knees and thighs. After half a mile it becomes (I am not exaggerating) an unbearable agony.

As well as Wigan, Orwell visited the towns of Sheffield and Barnsley, touring slum houses as well as mines, and talking to people about their work and political beliefs. With *The Road to Wigan Pier,* he began to define his politics, with particular reference to socialism. His vexed relationship to this political philosophy was to influence his writing and ideas for the rest of his career. Socialism was particularly popular among intellectuals of the 1930s. It involved the belief that property, land, and the means of production that control the economy should be owned by the community in general, rather than by individuals or by corporations. This system would lead to the abolition of class distinctions and a more just society, socialists believed, since power and money would be no longer in the hands of the few but shared by all.

Orwell abhorred the existing class system, but he did not believe that class distinctions could easily be eliminated. He supported socialism in the abstract, but critiqued middle-class socialists for believing that a classless society could be achieved by merely changing the economic system: "To abolish class distinctions means abolishing part of yourself. It is not enough to clap a proletarian on the back and tell him he is as good a man as you are." He felt that many intellectuals were hypocrites who spoke in idealistic terms and were unaware of the realities of the situations they condemned.

Orwell's critique of middle-class socialists in *The Road to Wigan Pier* was quite harsh—so harsh that Gollancz ended up writing an apologetic preface to the book. He was well aware that the intended audience of the book was the very people that Orwell was attacking. Gollancz countered Orwell's critique by pointing out the writer's own contradictions: "He is a frightful snob still, and a genuine hater of every form of snobbery." Orwell may never have fully overcome his feelings of difference from the working-class people he met. But unlike many, he was honest about his feelings and aware that his inconsistencies posed problems for his desire for social justice.

Despite Gollancz's fears about the book, it proved to be a great success with both members of the Left Book Club and numerous other readers. By the time it was published in 1937, however, Orwell had already moved on to a new stage of his life. His first copy of the book was sent to him in the trenches of war-torn Spain, where he was actively fighting for the socialist cause he had recently finished writing about.

This anarchist poster from the first months of the Spanish Civil War depicts a revolutionary worker fighting the serpent of fascism; in contrast to the treachery of the snake, the man's nudity reflects the purity of his cause.

IN THE TRENCHES

War broke out in Spain in July 1936. The struggle was between forces on opposite ends of the political spectrum. A revolutionary group of Leftists, made up of socialists, communists, and anarchists, had recently managed to oust Spain's repressive conservative government and establish a new administration that supported the working class. The new government was known as the Republican Party, or Popular Front. The different parties that made up the Republicans were drawn together by the workers, and their conflicting goals would later create new problems for Spain. The socialists and anarchists had the most in common: They both saw themselves as revolutionary parties that wanted to change the structure of society immediately, and set up a worker's state. The communists, on the other hand, were more inclined to follow orders from the Communist Party in Russia, and wanted to postpone revolutionary change until after the new government had settled in. Temporarily, though, the parties coexisted harmoniously and the new government was widely celebrated by the Spanish workers.

Before long, however, the Right had organized a reaction in the form of a military coup, led by General

Francisco Franco. He and his followers, a mix of traditional conservatives and Fascists, intended to dismantle Spain's social revolution and establish an authoritarian state. Fellow Fascist leaders Adolf Hitler of Germany and Benito Mussolini of Italy supported Franco in his efforts. Intellectuals around the world responded by supporting the Republican cause against the Fascists. Fascism, a political movement that spread across Europe during the 1930s, drew on strong nationalistic feeling and encouraged leader-worship. It was seen as the antithesis of democracy: a frightening trend that must be stopped at all costs. Britain and France, however, were unwilling to go to war on behalf of the Republicans. They did not want to support a party that represented the workers, for fear that their own workers would revolt. In the end, not a single country sent armies to Spain to help defeat Franco.

Individually, though, a great many people were willing to fight on behalf of the Spanish Republic. It was an unprecedented event—more than 40,000 young people, from more than 50 nations, offered to fight and die for a cause outside of their own country. A combination of intellectuals and workers, the volunteers were united by a sense of solidarity with Spain's new democracy, and by their fear of Fascism. Two thousand volunteers came from Britain, and one of them was Orwell.

Orwell believed in the fight against Fascism, but he was not sure what his role in the war would be. He knew he wanted to write about the struggle, but was not convinced that he had the necessary experience to serve in the Republican army. He scraped together the funds to travel to Spain by pawning the Blair family silver; Eileen later told Orwell's mother that the silver was missing because it had been sent away for engraving.

In order to present himself as a sympathizer in Spain, he needed a letter of introduction from a political group in England that supported the Republican cause. He finally

obtained one from the Independent Labour Party (ILP), a group that identified itself with a division of the Republicans, known as POUM (in Spanish, the initials stood for the "Workers' Party for Marxist Unification"). POUM was the most revolutionary and independent of all the groups aligned against Franco. Without really knowing what he was getting involved in, Orwell committed himself to working with POUM once he got to Spain.

On his way across Europe, Orwell stopped briefly in Paris, where he met the American writer and expatriate Henry Miller. Miller warned him that going to Spain was a reckless and dangerous move, but Orwell was not deterred. Later, he recalled this conversation with Miller in one of his most famous essays, "Inside the Whale," a review of Miller's writing in which he contemplates the relationship between writers and their politics.

Orwell rode into Spain on a train packed with a diverse group of volunteers, including Czech, German, and French people, among others. He was touched by the camaraderie

Standing at the very rear of the column, Orwell towers over his neighbors in the ranks of the POUM militia, Barcelona, January 1937.

These Spanish Civil War soldiers were hot at midday, but Orwell remembered the nights being very cold: "Our miserable mountain had not even at its best much vegetation, and for months it had been ranged over by freezing militiamen, with the result that everything thicker than one's finger had long since been burnt."

among these young soldiers-to-be and by the support they received along the way. Peasants working in fields alongside the tracks paused to salute the volunteers as the train passed by.

When they finally arrived in Barcelona, Orwell was still more impressed by what he witnessed there. In *Homage to Catalonia*—his nonfiction book about the Spanish war—he described his awe at how the revolutionary government had transformed society: "You saw very few conspicuously destitute people, and no beggars except the gypsies. Above all, there was a belief in the revolution and the future, a feeling of having suddenly emerged into an era of equality and freedom."

The harmonious atmosphere extended to interpersonal relationships as well: "How easy it was to make friends in Spain! Within a day or two there was a score of militiamen who called me by my Christian name, showed me the ropes, and overwhelmed me with hospitality." He was particularly struck by his encounter with a young Italian soldier. Though they barely spoke two words to each other, Orwell felt a deep connection with the boy. In an essay entitled simply "Looking Back on the Spanish War," he summed up what the soldier's shabby uniform and fierce but vulnerable face had meant to him: "The central issue of the war was the attempt of people like him to win the decent life which they knew to be their birthright."

Though he had thought that he might not make good soldier material, Orwell's observations of the militias soon taught him otherwise. Most of the soldiers were so young and badly trained that he actually had more experience than they did thanks to his police service in India. Rather than merely observe as a journalist, he decided to join the POUM militia. The new government had wrought changes there as well. Rank and hierarchy had been abolished, and Orwell noted that the troops were willing to follow orders because they wanted to, not because they were forced to.

Orwell soon became one of those giving orders. Among the few with the know-how to direct the inexperienced but enthusiastic POUM soldiers, he quickly made *capo,* or corporal. But it was a difficult job; the militia was a ragtag bunch, and Orwell was initially appalled by their incompetence. In *Homage to Catalonia,* he recalled that "this mob of eager children, who were going to be thrown into the front line in a few day's time, were not even taught how to fire a rifle or pull the pin out of a bomb. At the time I did not grasp that this was because there were no weapons to be had."

The artillery for his troop was particularly pitiful, with an average of one machine gun per 50 men. In addition to their meager supplies, each troop was equipped with a single, mangy dog as a mascot: "One wretched brute that marched with us had had POUM branded on it in huge letters and slunk along as though conscious that there was something wrong with its appearance." The troops were lacking not only in weapons but also in the discipline and training to use them, and the first victims of the weapons were often their owners. On more than one occasion, Orwell witnessed a POUM injury caused by the clumsy mishandling of a weapon.

The lack of weapons and training was not the only surprise in store for Orwell. He had yet to discover the unorthodox methods the troops used to "attack" the enemy. Since there were so few weapons to be had, the POUM soldiers worked on destroying enemy morale and winning converts by shouting slogans at the Fascists from behind their trenches. Orwell was astonished at this tactic: "The idea of trying to convert your enemy instead of shooting him!" Later, however, he admitted that it did seem to win them extra soldiers. The slogans yelled at the enemy varied from insults and revolutionary sentiments, to vivid descriptions of how much better off the POUM soldiers were than the Fascists. *Homage to Catalonia* provides a humorous example of how the POUM slogan-shouter operated: "His account of the Government rations was apt to be a little imaginative. 'Buttered toast!'—you could hear his voice echoing down the lonely valley—'We're just sitting down to buttered toast over here! Lovely sliced buttered toast.'"

Orwell was on the battlefront for four months, where his enthusiasm and teaching skills made him immensely popular with the troops. His ability to learn languages quickly—a crucial skill in an army made up of so many different nationalities—contributed to his success. Stafford Cottman, an English soldier who fought alongside him, remembered Orwell as the best-liked man in the whole contingent, and the ILP's publication, the *New Leader,* cited him for heroic behavior.

War was not all heroics, however. Orwell spent endless, dreary hours in the bone-chilling cold waiting for weapons, commands from headquarters, or enemy movement. He passed the time smoking thick tobacco and reciting poetry to himself to relieve his boredom. Writing was also a source of relief. All of his experiences were recorded in detail in his diary, later to serve as material for *Homage to Catalonia*. A welcome break in the daily routine of soldiering finally came in the form of a visit from his wife.

Eileen had applied for a job as a secretary at ILP headquarters in Barcelona. As soon as she heard that she had been accepted, she left the cottage in Wallington in the care of Orwell's Aunt Nellie, and made her way to Spain. Upon arrival, she set herself up at the Hotel Continental, and at the first opportunity visited Orwell at the front. During her visit, Orwell's troop weathered a Fascist bombardment, which Eileen later said she found quite exciting. She was pleased to be near her husband again, and in a position to support his cause. Back in Barcelona, she put together

A visit from Eileen was welcome relief from the drudgery of soldiering at the Aragon front in the spring of 1937. Orwell is sixth standing from the right; Eileen is sitting in front of him.

packages of tobacco and books and shipped them to the front. Once, when Orwell was forced to stay at a small, unpleasant hospital in Monflorite because of a hand infection, she managed to smuggle him a box of cigars.

Following his hospital stay, Orwell took part in the most serious phase of fighting thus far: a raid on the enemy's position at the Aragon front. One of fifteen volunteers who had agreed to lead the raid, he soon found himself flat in the mud, caught between the enemy's fire and that of his troops. It was a hair-raising episode, and one that he was lucky to survive. Yet even in the grimmest days of fighting, near-death experiences, and crawling through rain and mud, he was able to find redeeming features in his surroundings. In his account of the raid, he noted: "Wild roses with pink blooms the size of saucers straggle over the shell-holes around Torre Fabian. Behind the line you met peasants wearing wild roses over their ears. In the evenings they used to go out with green nets, hunting quails."

Orwell was a relatively fearless soldier, by all accounts, but the war did bring him face-to-face with his biggest phobia—rats. Just like his character Winston in *Nineteen Eighty-four*, Orwell loathed the large rodents and constantly found himself in situations where he could not escape them. Once, he and his troops were holed up in a rotting barn where "the floor was a thin layer of chaff over deep beds of bones, human bones and cows' bones mixed up, and the place was alive with rats. The filthy brutes came swarming out of the ground on every side." He was appalled by the sensation of the animals running over him in the dark, but managed to punch one of them as it scuttled by, sending it flying through the air. Robert Edwards, one of the ILP leaders at the front, recalled an episode in which Orwell resorted to his gun to deal with a particularly aggressive rat, and ended up triggering a barrage of enemy gunfire. A cookhouse and two buses were destroyed in the incident.

In April 1937, Orwell took a brief leave from the front. He was hugely relieved, for he would now have the chance to rid himself of another wartime pest—the lice that had become an unbearable part of his daily life. In *Homage to Catalonia,* his tirade against this particular brand of vermin demonstrates the degree to which he had come to loathe them: "For sheer beastliness the louse beats everything I have encountered....The human louse somewhat resembles a tiny lobster, and he lives chiefly in your trousers. Short of burning all your clothes there is no known way of getting rid of him."

Orwell returned to Barcelona with the intention of using his leave time to apply to fight with the prestigious International Brigade on the Madrid front. When he arrived, however, he realized that the political situation had changed dramatically. The Republican revolution was in retreat, and divisions between rich and poor were again evident on the streets. The unity of the left-wing groups against Franco had begun to weaken, while the government members who had initially supported the workers' parties were slowly but surely becoming more conservative. Eventually, fighting broke out between the anarchists and the government, and before Orwell's astonished eyes, barricades went up and gunshots broke out all over the city.

Orwell had initially refused to take sides among the different parties that formed

This war poster, released by the Ministry of Propaganda in Madrid, attempted to rally international support against Franco by depicting the destruction that the war was wreaking on everyday lives. To Orwell's dismay, no European country ever came to the aid of the Republicans.

the Republican alliance. He believed that they all supported substantially the same goal: defeating the Fascists. Now, however, he realized that the communists had turned against his own group, POUM. The reasons for this were complicated. Communists typically stood for social revolution, as did POUM. Now, however, Russia's communist leader, Joseph Stalin, was advising the Spanish communists that they were not yet ready for revolution. In accordance with his advice, they began to modify their political goals. Furious when POUM refused to do the same, the communists began to accuse them of treachery. What it came down to, Orwell later wrote, was that Russia was worried about jeopardizing its relations with France, which did not want revolution fermenting on its borders in neighboring Spain. "The clue to the behavior of the Communist party in any country," he wrote bitterly, "is the military relation of that country, actual or potential, towards the U.S.S.R."

Orwell watched the street war in Barcelona from the roof of POUM headquarters, where he was assigned to keep watch. He read paperbacks to while away the time, and marveled at what he called "the folly of it all." He was not only bored, but angry and frustrated too. POUM had now been accused of instigating the street-fighting and of being in cahoots with the Fascist Right, when in fact they were one of the only remaining groups that clung to the idea of a left-wing revolution.

Soon, injury was added to insult. On May 20, 1937, back at the front, Orwell peered over the sandbag on top of his trench and was hit in the throat by a sniper's bullet. He fell backwards, numb and dazed, hitting his head on the ground. In *Homage to Catalonia,* he remembered the experience vividly:

> Roughly speaking it was the sensation of being at the centre of an explosion. There seemed to be a loud bang and a blinding flash of light all around me, and I felt a tremendous shock—no pain, only a violent shock, such

as you get from an electric terminal; with it a sense of utter weakness, a feeling of being stricken and shrivelled up to nothing.

He was immediately carried to the clinic at Monflorite, where he was injected with morphine to dull the pain, then transported to a larger hospital at Barbastro. There, the doctors informed him that the bullet had missed his spine and a main artery, but by only a millimeter. One of his vocal chords was paralyzed, however, and for a short time he was virtually unable to talk. His friend and fellow soldier Georges Kopp noted that his sense of humor remained untarnished by the incident, but that his voice sounded like "the characteristic, grinding noise of the brakes of a model T, very antiquated, Ford; his speech was inaudible outside a range of two yards."

After a few days, Orwell was back on his feet, wobbly but intact. He was discharged from the hospital and spent his newfound freedom being shuttled from one place to another while his discharge papers were prepared. He was no longer fit for military service and felt useless and depressed as a result. There was little to do but observe the goings-on around him with a wry detachment: "I watched a man making a skin bottle and discovered with great interest, what I had never known before, that they are made with the fur inside and the fur is not removed, so that you are really drinking distilled goat's hair. I had drunk out of them for months without knowing this." Eventually, his papers appeared and he made his way back to Barcelona to rejoin his wife.

At the Hotel Continental, Eileen was waiting for him in the lobby. She immediately approached him, put her arm around his neck affectionately, and hissed into his ear "Get out!" Hurriedly, she maneuvered her confused husband outside the hotel and explained what had happened. The counter-revolution was in full force, and POUM was its chief scapegoat. Its members were being arrested and thrown into jail. Already, POUM's leader, Andrés Nin, was under arrest, as was their friend Georges Kopp. Orwell's hotel room had been searched in his absence, and all their papers confiscated, with the lucky exception of their passports and some checks. These had been hidden under the bed, which Eileen was lying on when the police burst in to search the room. Orwell later said that it was probably their Spanish chivalry that prevented them from removing her to check underneath it.

It was clear that Orwell could not stay at the hotel a moment longer. They decided that Eileen would remain there, since she had been left alone thus far, while Orwell would go into hiding. Again, the writer was "down and out," sleeping on the streets and living by his wits. His first night on the streets of Barcelona found him sleeping in the ruins of a church that had been destroyed in the war. In the daytime, he and Eileen would pose as British travelers. In *Homage to Catalonia,* Orwell described the time as "an extraordinary, insane existence" that demanded a dual identity: "By night we were criminals, but by day we were prosperous English visitors—that was our pose, anyway. Even after a night in the open, a shave, a bath, and a shoeshine do wonders with your appearance."

Orwell, by now, was furious. The POUM suppression, led chiefly by the communists, was a betrayal of the Left by its own members that greatly weakened the fight against Fascism. He took out his frustration on his surroundings: "The passage-ways of several smart restaurants had '*Visca POUM*' [Long live POUM] scrawled on them as large as I could write it." Initially, he was more angered than frightened by the situation, for he was sure he had done nothing wrong. When a friend of his died in jail, however, he realized that his innocence would not protect him, and that he must flee the country as soon as possible.

On June 23, 1937, the Orwells, accompanied by John McNair, the ILP leader, posed as tourists and boarded a train heading north. They read novels and tried desperately to look nonchalant. Once over the border, they embraced in open relief. Their relief was well warranted, for the first Spanish newspaper they saw on arrival in France announced that John McNair had been arrested for spying. Clearly, the police had intended his capture for the night of their escape, and had prematurely declared victory to the press.

Orwell returned to England after a brief, depressing holiday in France, profoundly disillusioned. At home, left-wing sympathizers with the Republican war effort had tended to follow Stalin's party line, and had criticized the POUM faction in the press. Orwell was particularly angered at these critics because they had written about the war from the safety of their homes and newspaper offices, without facts or experience to back up their claims. He expressed his anger by writing an article on communist hypocrisy and submitting it to a journal that he had written for in the past, the *New Statesman,* but it was promptly rejected.

He faced similar problems trying to publish the full story of his experience, *Homage to Catalonia,* which was ready for publication in 1938. His regular publisher, Victor Gollancz, like other left-wingers at the time, did not wish to be associated with anything that appeared to criticize the fight against Fascism. Orwell's point was that the communists were now using Fascist methods to suppress others— that the fight against Fascism had become Fascist itself. But his views were met only by censorship and criticism. This suppression of his version of the truth was a grim awakening, and one that was later to influence his novel *Nineteen Eighty-four,* which depicts a world where the truth is constantly stifled and lies are fed to the public on a daily basis.

All was not completely lost, however. Fredric Warburg, founder of a small publishing company called Secker and Warburg, had heard about Orwell's controversial analysis of left-wing politics and found his viewpoint intriguing. He

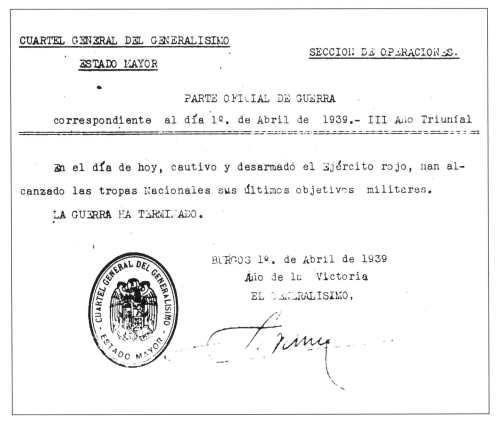

CUARTEL GENERAL DEL GENERALISIMO   SECCION DE OPERACIONES.

  ESTADO MAYOR

     PARTE OFICIAL DE GUERRA

correspondiente al día 1º. de Abril de 1939.- III Año Triunfal

  En el día de hoy, cautivo y desarmado el Ejército rojo, han alcanzado las tropas Nacionales sus últimos objetivos militares.

  LA GUERRA HA TERMINADO.

        BURGOS 1º. de Abril de 1939
          Año de la Victoria
          EL GENERALISIMO,

In this communiqué, broadcast all over Spain on April 10, 1939, Franco declared "Today, the Red Army being disarmed and imprisoned, the Nationalist troops have reached their final military objectives. The war has ended."

actively solicited Orwell's book and offered him 150 pounds for it. Thus, *Homage to Catalonia* was finally available in print. Sadly for Orwell, it did not do well. Though his account of the Spanish Civil War became immensely influential in later years, it was published to largely negative reviews in the repressive climate of the 1930s and sold badly. Orwell had a greater disappointment to contend with, however. Back at their cottage in Wallington, he and his wife followed the news in horror as the Fascists finally defeated the divided forces of the Spanish revolution.

  Although Orwell was crushed by this defeat, he did reach a new understanding of his contribution. In the face of hypocrisy on every side of the political spectrum, he was determined to use his writing to speak out against injustice wherever he saw it. As a result, he became one of the first of his generation to see and openly denounce the totalitarian tendencies of Stalin's Russia. The ending of *Homage to Catalonia,* which spoke of England's "deep sleep" being awakened by the sound of bombs, was both disturbing and prophetic, coming as it did on the eve of World War II.

But Orwell's vision after his Spanish experience was not entirely a dark one. His belief in social justice remained unwavering. Despite his disappointment in the behavior of the Left, he remained inspired by what he had seen in his brightest moments in Spain: "One had been in a community where hope was more normal than apathy or cynicism, where the word 'comrade' stood for comradeship and not, as in most countries, for humbug. One had breathed the air of equality."

Orwell lived through the destruction in London during the Blitz, after which this photograph was taken. His diary entry for September 7 read: "Noise of bombs and gunfire, except when very close (which probably means within two miles) now accepted as normal background to sleep or conversation."

FROM THE BLITZ
TO THE BBC

The threat of Fascism was not confined to Spain. As Orwell returned to England in 1937, a larger war was brewing. Hitler's ambitions in Europe were on the verge of provoking the largest armed conflict in human history: World War II. Rumors of an upcoming war faded in and out of the daily news reports. Orwell was uncertain of his reaction to this turn of events. His experience in Spain had left him suspicious of all political parties and their leaders, and had led him to believe that pacifism—the idea that war should be avoided at all costs—was the only legitimate philosophy. He found both the threat of the Nazis and the prospect of participating in another war equally repellent.

Orwell did not have much time to mull over the worsening political situation. A South African editor named Desmond Young had offered him a position as a writer for his journal *Pioneer,* based in Lucknow, India. Young had encountered Orwell's writing and found him to be "the best writer in England since Somerset Maugham." Excited at this new opportunity for travel and adventure, Orwell was ready to take the job. Then, all too suddenly, his health problems caught up with him. He had been sickly since boyhood, but his health was now deteriorating at an alarming rate in the aftermath of his bullet wound and strenuous activities in Spain. Moreover, he was suffering from frequent bouts of bronchitis. No sooner had he begun preparations to go to India than he was overcome by a severe coughing episode that produced alarming quantities of blood. He was rushed to a sanatorium in Kent where he was to remain for almost six months. One of the doctors there was Laurence O'Shaughnessy, Eileen's brother. An eminent lung specialist, O'Shaughnessy kept Orwell under close observation, for he believed that the writer might be suffering from tuberculosis—a potentially fatal disease at the time. His suspicion was confirmed when a tubercular lesion (a type of internal wound) was discovered on Orwell's lung.

During his mandatory rest period in the sanatorium, Orwell's health gradually improved. Once his lesion began to heal, he was allowed to leave on the condition that he take good care of himself. The doctors recommended that he do this by vacationing in a dry, hot climate. Perpetually poor, Orwell would not have been able to afford to escape England's damp weather, but for an unexpected act of generosity. L. H. Myers, a novelist, had recently met Orwell and immediately warmed toward him. On hearing of his financial predicament, Myers sent Orwell an anonymous gift of money through their mutual friends Max and Dorothy Plowman. Orwell did not want to accept the money as "charity," but agreed to regard it as a loan. True to his word, he repaid his mysterious benefactor through Dorothy Plowman as soon as he began to make money from his first financially successful novel, *Animal Farm*.

In September 1938, the Orwells left for Morocco. Again they left the house in Wallington in the hands of a caretaker—this time Orwell's friend and fellow writer Jack Common—and headed south. On their arrival, they found themselves a seedy hotel in Marrakech, which they later discovered was a brothel. Before long, however, they were able to settle more comfortably in a large villa, where they kept a garden complete with goats. Both Orwell and Eileen spent their days occupied in sedentary activities. They discussed politics and wrote avidly, recording their perceptions of Morocco. Occasionally the couple explored the surrounding areas. Once, they journeyed through the Atlas mountains, where they visited the Berber villages that dotted the hillsides. Orwell also worked on his newest novel. Not coincidentally, it was about a man taking a vacation from the regular routine of his life; he called it *Coming Up for Air.*

Though Eileen found aspects of the scenery beautiful, it was impossible to ignore the desperate poverty that pervaded Marrakech. Her diary shows her unable to romanticize her surroundings: "I found an open space to watch the sunset from and too late realised that part of the ground to the west...was a graveyard."

Though he was writing productively and getting the rest he needed, Orwell found his lifestyle monotonous and Morocco itself very depressing. The desolate landscape and the endless spectacle of poverty particularly dispirited him. In an essay about his trip, "Marrakech," he described how death had become a part of his everyday life there. A graveyard was situated behind their hotel, and so many old burial plots had been left untended that he and Eileen often found themselves walking over shallow graves. One day, they saw a dead body being carried past their hotel as they ate breakfast on the porch; Orwell remembered, "As the corpse went past the flies left the restaurant table in a cloud and rushed after it, but they came back a few minutes later." In a letter to a friend, Eileen noted Orwell's grim moods; he habitually spent the days speculating about the oncoming war and the potential calamities that might accompany it. His pessimism did not affect the progress of his writing, though, and six months after their arrival, Orwell was ready to return to England with a finished manuscript.

Orwell and Eileen set sail from Casablanca on a Japanese ship. Orwell typed the manuscript of *Coming Up for Air* on the voyage, and had it ready to hand over to

In Marrakech, 1939, Orwell spent much of his time writing at his desk.

Victor Gollancz the day they arrived. Though the publisher had rejected Orwell's last book on political grounds, he had a contract with the author and was willing to consider any new work he produced. The new novel reflected Orwell's fear for the future. It depicted an England on the verge of destruction, and looked back nostalgically at a past of tranquil summers in the country, similar to those of Orwell's own childhood. It also experimented with the idea of writing for the "man on the street," rather than for a highbrow audience, as a way of putting his socialist ideals into practice.

In keeping with this idea, its central character, George Bowling, is distinctly average—a middle-aged insurance salesman—but nonetheless worthy of note. The novel's title reflects the feeling of freedom experienced by Bowling after he decides to "come up for air" and go on a much-needed vacation. In Lower Binfield, the countryside of his childhood, Bowling thinks he will be able to find respite from the general bleakness of England's grim prewar environment and escape the boredom of his humdrum existence. Flight turns out to be useless, however, for Bowling learns that "War's in the air we breathe. The old life's finished. There's no way back to Lower Binfield." Like Orwell's later novels, *Coming Up for Air* was at once prophetic (in its vision of coming war) and bleak. Orwell was not as pessimistic as his writing, however; through it, he hoped to incite his audience to change the potentially grim future that he foresaw.

Another notable feature of the novel was a passage that bitingly satirized Gollancz's Left Book Club. Orwell was curious to see whether his former publisher would balk at publishing views divergent from his own, as he had with *Homage to Catalonia*. Gollancz did hesitate before publishing the novel, but then decided to go ahead with it. It came out on June 12, 1939. Unlike his memoir of Spain, Orwell's new novel sold quite well and earned him some of his best reviews to date.

Orwell began to write increasingly prolifically. He did not limit himself to novels, but wrote reviews, articles, and essays of criticism as well. One of these essays, about the novelist Charles Dickens, later became famous. Simply called "Dickens," it celebrated the Victorian writer's moral criticism of society and his ability to appeal to a wide array of readers, qualities that clearly mirrored Orwell's own objectives. What was notable about the essays that Orwell was now producing frequently was the fact that he was shunning the terms and categories of traditional criticism. Just as he wanted to write for ordinary people, he also chose to write interpretations of ordinary subjects. Essays such as those he wrote about cartoon postcards, detective novels, and weekly boys' magazines purposely ignored the distinctions commonly made between "high" and "low" forms of culture.

Orwell was one of the first critics to observe that these popular art forms were as worthy of notice as "serious" works of literature. He wrote about the way in which, just like literature, they followed certain conventions and influenced people's beliefs. In his essay "Boys' Weeklies," for instance, he argued that the magazines created a fantasy world in which "Everything is safe, solid and unquestionable. Everything will be the same for ever and ever." The magazines allowed one to forget the problems of modern life, for they created a world in which "The clock has stopped at 1910. Britannia rules the waves, and no one has heard of slumps, booms, unemployment, dictatorship, purges or concentration camps."

Though Orwell's reputation as a writer and critic was growing steadily, he had other things on his mind. World War II had begun and was an unavoidable fact of daily life. Though Orwell had initially opposed the idea of going to war, he soon came to change his mind. When the Stalin-Hitler pact was announced in August 1939, he decided that the enemy was far more dangerous than any leaders he distrusted in Britain, and that he must fight for his country against the forces of Fascism. He justified his position in an essay entitled "My Country Right or Left," which called for a combination of patriotism and socialism. If you want to change your country, he argued, you should be prepared to defend it first.

Orwell's newfound patriotism was destined to be frustrated. He volunteered for the armed forces but was not enlisted to fight because of his poor health. Meanwhile, Eileen had left the cottage in Wallington to participate in the war effort by working for the Ministry of Censorship. With Eileen away in London, serving the war without him, Orwell felt lonely and ineffectual. He passed the time by planting potatoes to store in case of a war famine. He was not the most experienced farmer, however, and when he dug up the potatoes to store them, he found that they had already grown moldy. Determined that he must begin to experience the war properly, along with his wife and the rest of London, he closed up the farm and set off for the capital.

Still relatively poor, Orwell and Eileen moved together to a meager apartment on Chagford Street, located on the top floor of a house—the most dangerous place to live in the event of a bomb raid. Orwell tried again to enlist, only to be disappointed a second time. In a diary entry from June 1940, he wrote: "Horribly depressed by the way things are turning out. Went this morning for my medical board and was turned down, my grade being C in which they aren't at present taking any men in any corps."

He had little choice now but to live by his writing. A position as film and theater critic for a periodical called *Time and Tide* was available, and, attracted to the idea of a regular salary, Orwell took it. He had never been a great fan of films, particularly American ones, and grumbled about how many of them he now had to see. It was clear that the job would not remain appealing to him for long. In the meantime, he staved off frustration by contributing articles on topics closer to his heart to a magazine called *Horizon,* run by his old friend from St. Cyprian's, Cyril Connolly. He also wrote occasionally for a left-wing newspaper called *Tribune.*

Before long, an appropriate outlet for his patriotism came along. The city of London had created a Home Guard—a volunteer citizen army that was to protect it in the event that Hitler invaded Britain—and Orwell signed up immediately. Because of his experience serving in Spain, he was made a sergeant in the Fifth London Battalion, a force of 20 men. Fredric Warburg, who had published *Homage to Catalonia,* was among the men serving under him. Orwell tried to organize the Home Guard along the lines of the Spanish Militia, encouraging its members to think of themselves as a revolutionary People's Army, rather than just a defense force. Excited by this unexpected opportunity to fight and command, he suggested all kinds of guerrilla warfare techniques that could be used in the event of a German invasion.

This was the time of the infamous London Blitz, when German V1 dive-bombers conducted nightly raids on London, showering the city with bombs popularly known as "doodlebugs." Though the origin of this insect-like name is unclear, it may have been due to the eerie whistling noise they made as they fell: Because of this sound, they were also known as "buzz bombs." Highly destructive, the bombs killed thousands and left ten times as many homeless. Many

Londoners took up residence in the underground subway stations in an effort to escape them. Rather than retreating to the quiet of Wallington, where they would be safe from the relentless terror of the raids, Orwell and Eileen deliberately stayed on in London. Ever conscientious, they felt that it would be cowardly to leave while others had no choice but to face the bombs. They remained surprisingly calm throughout the surrounding mayhem. One day, Eileen telephoned Orwell from her brother's house and paused for a second during the phone conversation. When Orwell asked her what was wrong, she casually informed him that a bomb had just caused a window to explode. Another close shave was recorded in Orwell's war diary in a similarly offhand manner: "woken up by a tremendous crash, said to be caused by a bomb in Maida Vale. E and I merely remarked on the loudness and fell asleep again."

Eileen was soon to be directly affected by the war. Her brother Laurence was killed at the battle of Dunkirk and, to add to her suffering, her grief-stricken mother died shortly afterward. The Orwells were also contending with the visible suffering of those around them, which Orwell meticulously recorded in his diary, along with his observations of war-torn London. His characteristically stark language accented the daily horrors he witnessed:

> Passed this morning a side-street somewhere in Hampstead with one house in it reduced to a pile of rubbish by a bomb—a sight so usual that one hardly notices it. The street is cordoned off, however, digging squads at work, and a line of ambulances waiting. Underneath that huge pile of bricks there are mangled bodies, some of them perhaps alive.

Among these horrors, Orwell somehow managed to retain a journalist's eye for the incidental detail. One of his diary entries from July 1940 notes:

> This evening I saw a heron flying over Baker Street. But this is not so improbable as the thing I saw a week or

two ago, i.e. a kestrel killing a sparrow in the middle of Lord's cricket ground. I suppose it is possible that the war, i.e. the diminution of traffic tends to increase bird life in inner London.

The Orwells were also afflicted by insufficient funds. Though Orwell seldom complained out loud about his lack of money, he did confess in his diary on one occasion, "The money situation is becoming completely unbearable." The articles and reviews that he was now churning out at an impressive rate simply did not pay well. Yet his reputation continued to thrive. Through his forceful political articles, Orwell had made a name for himself as a spokesman for his own particular brand of socialism. His straightforward, confident writing style was particularly appealing to a public uncertain of the future and sick of hearing the same old arguments. As evidence of his growing popularity, a piece entitled "The Lion and the Unicorn: Socialism and the English Genius" sold approximately 12,000 copies. Another ardent declaration of the mutual aims of socialism and patriotism, it was later republished as *England Your England,* and is remembered as one of his most significant critical pieces.

The essay was published as the first in a pamphlet series called Searchlight Books, edited by Orwell himself, along with another writer, T. R. Fyvel. Fredric Warburg, whose firm published the series, had introduced the two writers, presuming their similar political views would give them a lot to say to each other. Fyvel and Orwell got along immediately and remained close for the duration of Orwell's life; Fyvel later published a personal memoir of his experiences as Orwell's colleague and friend. The series, however, had less staying power than the friendship. Warburg had hoped that it would serve as an ongoing way to provoke public debate about Fascism, but none of the succeeding pamphlets sold as well as "The Lion and the Unicorn" and the project was eventually abandoned.

Among other prestigious journalism assignments, Orwell was asked to write for the *Partisan Review,* an eminent American journal edited by the art critic Clement Greenberg. Orwell's writing became a regular feature in the journal, contributing a series of articles called "London Letter" that described the British political situation to the *Partisan Review*'s American audience. His enthusiasm for the column was somewhat dampened, however, when he discovered that his articles were subject to censorship by the British Ministry of Information (MOI), and that portions were cut and edited without his permission. With this revelation began Orwell's profound mistrust of the MOI, which he later satirized in *Nineteen Eighty-four* through his creation of the oppressive and sinister Ministry of Truth.

Orwell was to come into close contact with the MOI over the next several months. In 1941, he was offered a job as a radio broadcast assistant for the British Broadcasting Corporation (BBC). As a result of his experience in Burma,

Orwell (standing at left) records a session of the BBC poetry magazine "Voice" for broadcast to India. According to colleague John Morris, Orwell wrote beautiful broadcasts but delivered them in a flat, droning voice.

he was asked to work for the Indian Section of the BBC's Empire Service. The BBC, usually an impartial public corporation, was under the command of the MOI for the duration of the war, since radio broadcasting played a central role in the dissemination of wartime propaganda.

The Germans and their allies had begun broadcasting to India in an attempt to sabotage Britain's position in the war by exhorting the Indians to revolt against their British rulers. The BBC was commissioned to retaliate by projecting a positive image of British culture and Britain's role in the war. Because the broadcasts were seen as a vital function of British security, they were subject to two layers of censorship: The MOI approved all the scripts before they went on the air, and the BBC censors had the power to cut off a "disloyal" statement at the turn of a switch. All seemingly spontaneous broadcasts were in fact carefully checked and double-checked by the ministry's employees.

Orwell now found himself being better paid than he had been in years (his salary was 680 pounds per year, then an impressive figure); he was, however, also in an unfortunate position. His writing was again subject to scrutiny and censorship. Worse, his work involved circulating war propaganda and pro-imperial sentiment that he did not believe in. The entire venture, in fact, conflicted wildly with his belief in telling the truth at all times. Nonetheless, Orwell was willing to do it. He had wanted desperately to fight in the war, and if his broadcasting would somehow aid the victory effort he would swallow his pride and contribute the only way he could.

He was prepared for his new job by a six-week course in broadcasting at the Emergency Training School for BBC employees, affectionately known as "The Liars' School" by some of its graduates. Then it was on to the BBC.

The Eastern Services branch was housed at 200 Oxford Street, on the ground floor of a department store that had been commandeered by the BBC during the war. It was a

The two censor's stamps on this script for one of Orwell's radio talks on literature signify that it has been deemed suitable for broadcast. The talk is on Jack London, an American writer who, like Orwell, visited the slums of London disguised as one of the poor.

Rec.:March 1st St.6. 2.30 to 4. BST.

Friday, March 5th 1115-1145 GMT

(To be recorded 1.3.43)

B.B.C.
PASSED FOR SECURITY

LANDMARKS IN AMERICAN LITERATURE. No.5.
Talk on JACK LONDON. by George Orwell.

Jack London, like Edgar Allen Poe, is one of those writers who have a bigger reputation outside the English-speaking world than inside it - but indeed,

B.B.C.
PASSED FOR POLICY
DATE   SIGNATURE

more so than Poe, who is at any rate taken seriously in England and America, whereas most people, if they remember Jack London at all, think of him as a writer of adventure stories not far removed from penny dreadfuls.

Now, I myself don't share the rather low opinion of Jack London which is held in this country and America; and I can claim to be in good company, for another admirer of Jack London's work was no less a person than Lenin, the central figure of the Russian Revolution. After Lenin's death his widow, Nadeshda Krupskaya, wrote a short biography of him, at the end of which she describes how she used to read stories to Lenin when he was paralysed and slowly dying. On the last day of all, she says, she began to read him Dickens's "Christmas Carol", but she could see that he didn't like it; what she calls Dickens's "bourgeois sentimentality" was too much for him. So she changed over to Jack London's story "Love of Life", and that was almost the last thing that Lenin ever heard. Krupskaya adds that it is a very good story. It is a good story, and Here I want only to point to this rather queer conjunction between a writer of thrillers - stories about Pacific islands and the goldfields of the Klondike, and also about burglars, prizefighters and wild animals - and the greatest revolutionary of modern times. I don't know with certainty what

cramped and noisy space with a maze of adjacent cubicles from which the perpetual sound of conversations, dictation, typing, and rehearsals could be heard. John Morris, one of Orwell's co-workers at the radio station, worked in the booth next to his. He remembered that on more than one occasion, he had looked up from his desk to see Orwell standing in the space between their cubicles with a "crucified" expression on his face. "For God's sake, shut up," Orwell would tell him.

Along with the aggravating work conditions and the constant menace of censorship, Orwell was appalled at the immense waste of time and paper generated by the radio station's bureaucratic style of organization. In his diary, he described the BBC in distinctly unflattering terms: "Its atmosphere is something halfway between a girls' school and a lunatic asylum, and all we are doing at present is useless, or slightly worse than useless. Our radio strategy is even more hopeless than our military strategy."

The BBC experience was later to provide Orwell with ample material for his creation of *Nineteen Eighty-four*'s nightmarish bureaucratic world. The BBC's maze-like offices, the green felt it used on tables to reduce noise, and its basement canteen all appear as significant details in his portrait of *Nineteen Eighty-four*'s various fiendish ministries. "Miniform," the real-life abbreviation for the Ministry of Information, is echoed in the novel in the Ministry of Truth's abridged name, "Minitrue." And just as the MOI building towered over London to such an extent that Orwell could see it from his home, the Ministry of Truth is constantly visible to *Nineteen Eighty-four*'s central character, the doomed rebel Winston Smith.

For most of his time at the BBC, Orwell used his real name, Eric Blair. He felt that to do otherwise would mean compromising his literary reputation, over which he was determined to maintain control. He also pointed out to his employers that his writer's name was associated with the anti-imperialism of his novel *Burmese Days,* which conflicted with the BBC's agenda of advocating British rule in India. Throughout his tenure at the BBC, Orwell held onto his belief that India should be independent. But he justified his work by reasoning that if England lost the war, India would be even worse off. If that happened, India might end up being ruled by Germany or Japan, whereas there was the chance Britain would grant India independence after the war was won. Despite this rationalization, Orwell did try to remain somewhat independent from the government position he was meant to be advocating on the radio. At one point, he was asked to criticize Nehru and Gandhi—

The bad food and depressing atmosphere of the BBC canteen reputedly inspired Orwell's depiction of the office cafeteria in Nineteen Eighty-four.

the Indian independence leaders—and refused to follow orders. This was only one of several occasions when he openly defied the BBC censors.

Although Orwell was deeply unsatisfied with his work, he was gaining a tremendous amount of writing experience. The job required him to produce a huge quantity of writing on a weekly basis. He often worked extremely long hours, going without sleep and then having to take time off from work due to fatigue. Part of his work involved producing weekly news reports on the war's progress. In order to write these reports, he waded through transcripts of the previous week's broadcasts from all around the world. He would then use the information to produce a news broadcast that favored England's position. Fascinated by the way that truth could be manipulated, Orwell started experimenting with the idea on his own. He started a rumor that beer was going to be rationed to see how long it would take the rumor to come back to him. Fortunately, it never did.

Orwell was also in charge of cultural programming for India. This part of his job was more rewarding, for it gave him the opportunity to work with interesting people and topics. He helped to organize a series of on-air discussions on the role of geography in the war—a subject that intrigued him and may have influenced his division of the world into three warring superpowers in *Nineteen Eighty-four*. "Voice," a live show featuring modern poets such as T. S. Eliot, was another of his innovative creations. Orwell's programming was not only creative but wide-ranging as well: English poetry, Indian plays, world politics, and classical music were all given air time. Even his wife was involved in the broadcasting. She had transferred from the Ministry of Censorship to the Ministry of Food, and took advantage of her new expertise by contributing recipes for breakfast to a program called "In Your Kitchen."

Orwell's BBC job forced him to sharpen his writing skills. He had to learn to write quickly and in a style that was well suited to radio: one that was clear, concise, and easy to follow. As a result, he was able to develop some of the best qualities of his writing. Whereas in the past Orwell would rework pieces multiple times before he was satisfied with them, journalism deadlines now forced him to learn to write accurately the first time around.

The subject matter he dealt with was also influential on his writing. One story he adapted for radio, "The Fox" by Ignazio Silone, undoubtedly affected his writing of *Animal Farm*, for it used a farm as a stage for Europe's political situation. Orwell later adapted *Animal Farm* itself for radio in 1946. Another source of inspiration was the topic of Basic English. An idea promoted during the war to ease communication among Britain's allies, Basic English involved reducing the number of words in the language until only the "basics" (850 words) were left. The idea of Newspeak—a highly condensed version of English—in *Nineteen Eighty-four* was clearly derived from Orwell's

ORWELL AND THE ENGLISH LANGUAGE

One of Orwell's most famous essays, "Politics and the English Language" called for a new level of clarity in the English language. Orwell believed that English had grown increasingly jargon-ridden, ambiguous, and corrupt in his time. Language corruption has political consequences, he believed, because "the slovenliness of our language makes it easier for us to have foolish thoughts." In his view, responsible political thinking would follow only from the responsible and careful use of language. A practical set of "rules" in the essay summed up how writers could begin to instill clarity and conciseness into the English language: Orwell tried diligently to follow these rules in his own writing, and his essays and novels are renowned for their unadorned and straightforward style.

    I. Never use a metaphor, simile, or other figure of speech which you are used to seeing in print.

    II. Never use a long word where a short one will do.

    III. If it is possible to cut a word out, always cut it out.

    IV. Never use the passive where you can use the active.

    V. Never use a foreign phrase, a scientific word, or a jargon word if you can think of an everyday English equivalent.

    VI. Break any of these rules sooner than say anything outright barbarous.

These rules sound elementary, and so they are, but they demand a deep change of attitude in anyone who has grown used to writing in the style now fashionable.

encounter with this strange idea. Significantly, Brendan Bracken, head of the Committee on Basic English, had the same initials as the novel's Big Brother.

The dishonesty and bureaucracy of the BBC continually frustrated Orwell. One of his diary entries from the time read: "We are all drowning in filth. When I talk to anyone or read the writing of anyone who has an axe to grind, I feel that intellectual honesty and balanced judgement have simply disappeared off the face of the earth." No one could tell the truth anymore, he felt, or even knew what it was. He began to take more risks with the censors, testing the limits of what he could do and say on the air. At the height of BBC censorship and propaganda, he hired Kingsley Martin, the editor of the *New Statesman,* to give a talk on— ironically—free speech. Not surprisingly, the program did not sit well with his supervisors.

Around this time, Orwell wrote a letter to a friend in which he announced that he had reached the end of his patience with the station, which was making him feel like "an orange that's been trodden on by a very dirty boot." In addition to the oppressive atmosphere, he had come across evidence that his work there was having little effect. A report showed that very few people in India were actually listening to the programming. The broadcasts' sound quality was poor and, confusingly for the audience, the shows were transmitted in different languages at different times (five Indian languages, as well as English, were used as part of the programming). Most important, only about one in 4,000 people in India actually owned a radio. In September 1943, Orwell handed in his resignation. The explanation he gave his employer was brief and to the point: "I am tendering my resignation because for some time past I have been conscious that I was wasting my own time and the public money on doing work that produces no result."

Orwell was not without resources after his resignation. Days after leaving the radio station, he was offered a position as the literary editor of the socialist newspaper *Tribune,* which he promptly accepted. The paper was the perfect antidote to his recent experience with the BBC. Orwell described it as "the one paper in England which had neither supported the government uncritically, nor opposed the war, nor swallowed the Russian myth." In other words, it was a publication whose politics were virtually identical to Orwell's. As he had done in the past, he tested the boundaries of what he could say by deliberately writing articles on seemingly frivolous topics like rose gardening, which he knew the hard-edged *Tribune* would see as snobbish and middle-class.

This installment of Orwell's Tribune *column, "As I Please," from 1944 is devoted to the topic of free speech in journalism, an ongoing concern of Orwell's in the censorial forties.*

JUNE 9, 1944.   TRIBUNE   13

AS I PLEASE: by George Orwell

ARTHUR KOESTLER'S recent article in *Tribune* set me wondering whether the book racket will start up again in its old vigour after the war, when paper is plentiful and there are other things to spend your money on.

Publishers have got to live, like anyone else, and you cannot blame them for advertising their wares, but the truly shameful feature of literary life before the war was the blurring of the distinction between advertisement and criticism. A number of the so-called reviewers, and especially the best known ones, were simply blurb writers. The "screaming" advertisement started some time in the nineteen-twenties, and as the competition to take up as much space and use as many superlatives as possible became fiercer, publishers' advertisements grew to be an important source of revenue to a number of papers. The literary pages of several well-known papers were practically owned by a handful of publishers, who had their quislings planted in all the important jobs. These wretches churned forth their praise—"masterpiece," "brilliant," "unforgettable" and so forth—like so many mechanical pianos. A book coming from the right publishers could be absolutely certain not only of favourable reviews, but of being placed on the "recommended" list which industrious book-borrowers would cut out and take to the library the next day.

If you published books at several different houses you soon learned how strong the pressure of advertisement was. A book coming from a big publisher, who had habitually spent large sums on advertisement, might get fifty or seventy-five reviews: a book from a small publisher might get only twenty. I knew of one case where a theological publisher, for some reason, took it into his head to publish a novel. He spent a great deal of money on advertising it. It got exactly four reviews in the whole of England, and the only full-length one was in a motoring paper, which seized the opportunity to point out that the part of the country described in the novel would be a good place for a motoring tour. This man was not in the racket, his advertisements were not likely to become a regular source of revenue to the literary papers, and so they just ignored him.

   * * *

EVEN reputable literary papers could not afford to disregard their advertisers altogether. It was quite usual to send a book to a reviewer with some such formula as: "Review this book if it seems any good. If not, send it back. We don't think it's worth while to print simply damning reviews."

Naturally, a person to whom the guinea or so that he gets for the review means next week's rent is not going to send the book back. He can be counted on to find something to praise, whatever his private opinion of the book may be.

In America even the pretence that hack-reviewers read the books they are paid to criticise has been partially abandoned. Publishers, or some publishers, send out with review copies a short synopsis telling the reviewer what to say. Once, in the case of a novel of my own, they misspelt the name of one of the characters. The same misspelling turned up in review after review. The so-called critics had not even glanced into the book—which, nevertheless, most of them were boosting to the skies.

   * * *

A PHRASE much used in political circles in this country is "playing into the hands of." It is a sort of charm or incantation to silence uncomfortable truths. When you are told that by saying this, that or the other you are "playing into the hands of" some sinister enemy, you know that it is your duty to shut up immediately.

For example, if you say anything damaging about British imperialism, you are playing into the hands of Dr. Goebbels. If you criticise Stalin you are playing into the hands of the *Tablet* and the *Daily Telegraph.* If you criticise Chiang-Kai-Shek you are playing into the hands of Wang Ching Wei—and so on, indefinitely.

Objectively this charge is often true. It is always difficult to attack one party to a dispute without temporarily helping the other. Some of Gandhi's remarks have been very useful to the Japanese. The extreme Tories will seize on anything anti-Russian, and don't necessarily mind if it comes from Trotskyist instead of right-wing sources. The American imperialists, advancing to the attack behind a smoke-screen of novelists, are always on the look-out for any disreputable detail about the British Empire. And if you write anything truthful about the London slums, you are liable to hear it repeated on the Nazi radio a week later. But what, then, are you expected to do? Pretend there are no slums?

Everyone who has ever had anything to do with publicity or propaganda can think of occasions when he was urged to tell lies about some vitally important matter, because to tell the truth would give ammunition to the enemy. During the Spanish civil war, for instance, the dissensions on the Government side were never properly thrashed out in the left-wing Press, although they involved fundamental points of principle. To discuss the struggle between the Communists and the Anarchists, you were told, would simply give the *Daily Mail* the chance to say that the Reds were all murdering one another. The only result was that the left-wing cause as a whole was weakened. The *Daily Mail* may have missed a few horror stories because people held their tongues, but some all-important lessons were not learned, and we are suffering from the fact to this day

Tribune passed the test and promised him the freedom to write on any topic he pleased. Appropriately, his column was called "As I Please," and it pursued a diverse range of topics. Anti-Americanism, irate taxi drivers, and bombing raids all served as subjects for Orwell's thoughtful speculations. At once literary and informal, political and self-indulgent, the column developed a wide following. Always expressive of Orwell's unique view of the world, it managed to upset readers on a regular basis. Its controversial nature only fueled its popularity.

Orwell was back in his old literary milieu. *Tribune* was located at the junction of Fleet Street and the Strand, near the offices of both of his book editors, Gollancz and Warburg. For lunch, he ate at the local Bodega wine bar, where he would debate politics and discuss upcoming column topics with friends and colleagues. He wrote steadily for a number of other publications as well, including the *Manchester Evening News, Horizon,* and the *New Statesman.* Soon the list also included one of England's oldest newspapers, the *Observer.* Cyril Connolly had introduced its editor, David Astor, to Orwell, and the two soon hit it off: Astor was eventually to become one of his closest friends. His time at the BBC and as a print journalist had provided him with valuable experience and wide exposure, and now he had found a home at *Tribune* as well. Orwell had finally come into his own.

"As I Please"

Orwell's column "As I Please," written periodically for the socialist newspaper Tribune *from 1943 to 1947, was one in which he had free rein to say whatever he "pleased" about topics of his own choice. He often took the opportunity to write about everyday subjects that applied to people's real-life problems and challenges. On February 9, 1945, he focused on the inefficiency of dishwashing, inspired, no doubt, by his own miserable experience of washing up for a living while working as a dishwasher in Paris. Here, he speculates on how modern technology might one day solve the problem of human drudgery. It is interesting to ponder how far, or not, we have caught up with Orwell's imagination.*

Every time I wash up a batch of crockery I marvel at the unimaginativeness of human beings who can travel under the sea and fly through the clouds, and yet have not known how to eliminate this sordid time-wasting drudgery from their daily lives. If you go into the Bronze Age room in the British Museum (when it is open again) you will notice that some of our domestic appliances have barely altered in three thousand years. A saucepan, say, or a comb, is very much the same thing as it was when the Greeks were besieging Troy. In the same period we have advanced from the leaky galley to the 50,000 ton liner, and from the ox–cart to the aeroplane.

It is true that in the modern labour-saving house in which a tiny percentage of human beings live, a job like washing-up takes rather less time than it used to. With soap flakes, abundant hot water, plate racks, a well-lighted kitchen, and—what very few houses in England have—an easy method of rubbish disposal, you can make it more tolerable than it used to be when copper dishes had to be scoured with sand in porous stone sinks by the light of a candle. But certain jobs (for instance, cleaning out a frying-pan which has had fish in it) are inherently disgusting, and this whole business of messing about with dishmops and basins of hot water is incredibly primitive. At this moment the block of flats I live in is partly uninhabitable: not because of enemy action, but because accumulations of snow have caused water to pour through the roof and bring down the plaster from the ceilings. It is taken for granted that this calamity will happen every time there is an exceptionally heavy fall of snow. For three days there was no water in the taps because the pipes were frozen: that, too, is a normal, almost yearly experience. And the newspapers have just announced that the number of burst pipes is so enormous that the job of repairing them will not be completed till the end of 1945—when, I suppose, there will be another big frost and they will all burst again. If our methods of making war had kept pace with our methods of keeping house, we should be just about on the verge of discovering gunpowder.

To come back to washing-up. Like sweeping, scrubbing and dusting, it is of its nature an uncreative and life-wasting job. You cannot make an art out of it as you can out of cooking or gardening. What, then, is to be done about it? Well, this whole problem of housework has three possible solutions. One is to simplify our way of living very greatly; another is to assume, as our ancestors did, that life on earth is inherently miserable, and that it is entirely natural for the average woman to be a broken-down drudge at the age of thirty; and the other is to devote as much intelligence to rationalizing the interior of our houses as we have devoted to transport and communications.

I fancy we shall choose the third alternative. If one thinks simply in terms of saving trouble and plans one's home as ruthlessly as one would plan a machine, it is possible to imagine houses and flats which would be comfortable and would entail very little work. Central heating, rubbish chutes, proper consumption of smoke, cornerless rooms, electrically warmed beds and elimination of carpets would make a lot of difference. But as for washing-up, I see no solution except to do it communally, like a laundry. Every morning the municipal van will stop at your door and carry off a box of dirty crocks, handing you a box of clean ones (marked with your initial of course) in return. This would be hardly more difficult to organize than the daily diaper service which was operating before the war. And though it would mean that some people would have to be full-time washers-up, as some people are now full-time laundry-workers, the all-over saving in labour and fuel would be enormous. The alternatives are to continue fumbling about with greasy dishmops, or to eat out of paper containers.

WAR IS PEACE
FREEDOM IS SLAVERY
IGNORANCE IS STRENGTH.

This manuscript page from a draft of Nineteen Eighty-four *features the infamous paradoxical Party slogans written in uppercase letters. After completing the first draft Orwell said, "about two thirds of it will have to be rewritten entirely besides the usual touching up."*

BECOMING A LEGEND

In 1944, Orwell decided that it was time to fulfill a different kind of ambition: becoming a father. He and Eileen had been unable to have a child of their own, and so far had lived too unsettled a life to think seriously of alternatives. Now that Orwell was more established and financially stable, he began to actively look into adoption. Gwen O'Shaughnessy, Eileen's sister-in-law, worked in a hospital and often heard of war orphans in need of good homes. Very soon, she had procured Orwell and Eileen a one-month-old baby boy, whom they named Richard Horatio Blair. Eileen had been less eager than Orwell to adopt. She was very busy with the Ministry of Food job and worried that she would not have the energy to take care of a child. She immediately fell in love with Richard, however, and even quit her job shortly after his arrival in order to spend more time with him.

The Orwells had recently moved across London to new, rather shabby quarters at 276 Canonbury Square. A bomb had landed on their apartment in Maida Vale, reducing it to little more than a pile of rubble, and they had been forced to seek new housing. Eileen later told a friend that they would probably have been able to afford a better place if they did not spend so much money on cigarettes. Despite the relative dinginess of their surroundings, Orwell and Eileen settled in quickly and entertained with some frequency. Their guests found them serenely happy, doting over their new son.

Despite Orwell's respect for *Tribune,* he found that there were drawbacks to working there. In addition to writing, his job entailed rejecting the work of struggling authors. This he found hard to do, having been one so recently himself, so he often ended up printing material that was not particularly good. As a result, would-be writers and reviewers who had heard that he was a sympathetic editor frequently besieged him. In 1945, relief came in the form of a job as European correspondent for the *Observer.* He accepted it without hesitation and handed his *Tribune* position over to his old friend T. R. Fyvel, complete with an entire desk full of unanswered correspondence from potential authors.

Because of his continued poor health, the trip to Europe was a potentially dangerous one, but Orwell was typically unconcerned about his own well-being. World War II was finally drawing to a close, and he was excited at the opportunity to observe its effects on the Continent. He was particularly curious to see the toll that Fascism had taken on Germany. In February 1945, he left for Paris. Once there, he stayed at the Hotel Scribe near the Opera and reported back to England on the movements of the Allies. The hotel, he wrote, was filled with American journalists boasting "stupendous salaries." One day Orwell noticed Ernest Hemingway's name on the hotel register, and went up to introduce himself to the famous American writer. Hemingway was as gruff and belligerent as Orwell had expected: Only after the awkward Englishman had made it clear that he was the writer George Orwell did Hemingway invite him in for a scotch. The hotel also housed the distinguished Oxford philosopher A. J. Ayer. The two became friendly and Ayer later bestowed high praise on Orwell in his memoirs by stating, "He was another of those whose liking for me made me think better of myself."

Orwell found the political situation in Paris disturbing. He was alarmed at the number of people who were being executed as traitors, and in his last two novels he drew on this experience of watching a community turn against its own members. From Paris he moved on to Cologne, Germany, where he was greeted by an equally disturbing spectacle. Large numbers of Germans were starving in the wake of their defeat, and many were displaced from their homes and families. Orwell had not expected to feel sorry for the people whom he had so recently thought of as the enemy, but he found that he did, and wrote an essay about the experience called "Revenge Is Sour." He was not in Germany long, however, before his health troubles landed him in a Cologne hospital.

His wife was to suffer a far worse fate. Eileen had written to him briefly to tell him she was going to have an operation. Tumors had been discovered inside her uterus, and an immediate hysterectomy was required. Although it was an urgent and life-saving operation, it was also considered a routine one, and the characteristically unruffled Eileen saw no need to worry her husband with details. Knowing how much he hated hospitals, she did not ask Orwell to return for the operation, and she even apologized for its cost. Tragically, the operation did not go according to plan. Eileen suffered an allergic reaction to the anesthetic and died suddenly on the operating table. Orwell was still in Cologne when the telegram arrived informing him of his loss.

Orwell was reduced to a state of shock. He checked out of the hospital and headed for home. There, a letter from Eileen awaited him. It had been written just before the operation, and to Orwell's relief it was cheerful and contained no premonition of what was about to happen to

her. In the days and months after Eileen's death, Orwell appeared strangely calm on the surface. In fact, he was deeply distraught, both for his own loss and that of his son. Though some of his friends expected him to give up Richard now that the boy would be motherless, Orwell remained deeply committed to his adopted son and was determined to raise him despite the difficulties.

Initially, though, he was unable to cope with the rhythms of ordinary life, and he returned to Europe to bury himself in his work, leaving Richard in the care of a friend. The early summer found him back in London, where he continued to use his writing as a panacea. That year, his first internationally successful novel, *Animal Farm,* was published. It was a mixed blessing. Glad as he was to see his new book in print, Orwell was saddened by the fact that Eileen could not share the success. In a letter to a friend, he wrote: "It was a terrible shame that Eileen didn't live to see the publication of *Animal Farm,* which she was particularly fond of and even helped in the planning of....[Her death] was a terribly cruel and stupid thing to happen."

The novel had been started much earlier, when Orwell first joined *Tribune* at the end of 1943. He wrote quickly, completing it within a few months. With this book more than any other, he had had a clear idea of what he wanted to say, and had come up with a captivating way to say it. Ever since his experience in Spain, he had been determined to undermine what he called the "Russian myth" and expose to the world the corruption of Stalin's regime. *Homage to Catalonia,* with its pitiful sales, had been a failure in this regard. But drawing on the experience of living in farm country in Wallington, and on his interest in children's fables, Orwell now came up with the idea of using the dynamics of a farmyard as a parable for the failure of the Russian Revolution. In *Animal Farm,* a book populated almost entirely by animals, a prize pig, Old Major, decides that it is time for animals to revolt against their masters and exploiters—the humans. Accordingly, the different barnyard animals unite and stage an insurrection against their farmer, Mr. Jones, triumphantly taking over the farm once they have driven the humans away. Initially, the revolution is a resounding success and the animals work diligently together to provide for themselves. Before long, however, the pigs begin to take over the farm and undo all the reforms the animals had worked for together, while craftily maintaining the myth that "all animals are equal." Boxer, the trusty old workhorse, is quietly sent to the glue factory and a new tyranny has soon replaced the old one.

To those familiar with recent history, Orwell's message was clear: The pigs represented the communist leaders, the faithful Boxer represented the working class, and the story's lesson was one the Russian people had suffered through. Readers of all ages, however, could appreciate the simple but poignant dynamics of this fairy-tale-like piece of

ANIMAL FARM

This extract from Animal Farm *depicts Snowball, the mastermind behind the pigs' takeover of the animals' revolution, practicing "doublethink" on the other animals. He reduces the "Seven Commandments," or principles of the revolution, to one banal precept, indicating the increasingly corrupt nature of the pigs' revolution and the gullibility of their followers.*

None of the other animals on the farm could get further than the letter A. It was also found that the stupider animals, such as the sheep, hens, and ducks, were unable to learn the Seven Commandments by heart. After much thought Snowball declared that the Seven Commandments could in effect be reduced to a single maxim, namely: "Four legs good, two legs bad." This, he said, contained the essential principle of Animalism. Whoever had thoroughly grasped it would be safe from human influences. The birds at first objected, since it seemed to them that they also had two legs, but Snowball proved to them that this was not so.

"A bird's wing, comrades," he said, "is an organ of propulsion and not of manipulation. It should therefore be regarded as a leg. The distinguishing mark of man is the hand, the instrument with which he does all his mischief."

The birds did not understand Snowball's long words, but they accepted his explanation, and all the humbler animals set to work to learn the new maxim by heart. FOUR LEGS GOOD, TWO LEGS BAD was inscribed on the end wall of the barn, above the Seven Commandments and in bigger letters. When they had once got it by heart, the sheep developed a great liking for this maxim, and often as they lay in the field they would all start bleating "Four legs good, two legs bad! Four legs good, two legs bad!" and keep it up for hours on end, never growing tired of it.

writing. With memorable slogans such as "Four legs good, two legs bad!" accenting his now-expert prose style, Orwell knew he had hit upon the perfect way to make both his writing and political ideas widely accessible.

Despite Orwell's confidence in his latest artistic vision and the fact that his ideas were now more clearly articulated than ever before, his new novel was dogged with problems. The manuscript was nearly destroyed by the bomb that had ruined his Maida Vale apartment, and it had to be rescued from the rubble. Moreover, his ideas were still considered very unfashionable. Along with many other intellectuals, Gollancz felt the need to support Stalin once the Hitler-Stalin pact had broken down and Russia had joined the British side in the war. He refused to publish a work that many would perceive as anti-Russian. As he had after his experience in Spain, Orwell found himself again in a position in which criticizing one side was equated with supporting the other. Anti-Stalinist sentiment, in other words, meant one was pro-Nazi, despite the fact that Orwell viewed both sides as equally undesirable fascists.

Orwell sent *Animal Farm* to several publishers, but word was out about the book's supposedly dangerous political content, and it was rejected again and again. Another problem was Gollancz's contract with Orwell; other publishers did not want to take on a potentially lucrative novelist only to have Gollancz capitalize on the success of the novel's sales with future books by the author. Immensely frustrated, Orwell briefly considered publishing it himself with the help of a loan from David Astor.

Instead, he made one last attempt to interest a publisher by approaching his former editor, Fredric Warburg, who had taken on the politically risky *Homage to Catalonia*. Orwell had not solicited Warburg initially because he believed that the publisher was suffering from drastic paper shortages, a common problem during the war. Later, Warburg remembered the clumsy way that Orwell approached him with

GEORGE ORWELL

ALE

WSZYSTKIE ZWIERZĘTA SĄ SOBIE RÓWNE I

NIEKTÓRE ZWIERZĘTA SĄ RÓWNIEJSZE od INNYCH.

FOLWARK ZWIERZĘCY

ORWELL
XF 50
ANI:POL

» ŚWIATPOL «

This Polish edition of Animal Farm, *printed in London in 1947, testifies to Orwell's widespread popularity outside the UK.*

the book. Thrusting the tattered manuscript at Warburg apologetically, Orwell informed him that he was bound to dislike it because it was too anti-Russian. In fact, Warburg liked it immensely, and instantly agreed to publish it.

Paper shortages were a factor, however, and delayed publication for several months. By the time Warburg was prepared to release the novel, the time was ripe for a positive reception. The war was now over, and Stalin was no longer an ally whose reputation needed to be defended. The novel did tremendously well, receiving glowing reviews from top British and American critics. The *New Yorker* hailed Orwell as a major writer, comparable to the great satirist Jonathan Swift, author of *Gulliver's Travels.* Not only was the book accessible, moving, and politically astute, but it was humorous as well—a trait that many found particularly appealing. The first printing of 4,500 sold out within two weeks, and over the next five years, tens of thousands of copies of the book were sold on both sides of the Atlantic. With the book's sale to the Book-of-the-Month Club in the United States, Orwell's financial success was assured.

Not everyone was charmed by *Animal Farm,* however. Some saw its portrayal of a doomed revolution as a pessimistic denial of the capacity for human change; others opportunistically used it as anti-Russian propaganda in the rapidly approaching Cold War with Russia. Still others misunderstood it completely—Orwell frequently stopped by bookstores to remove it from the children's shelves where it had been unwittingly placed by storeowners. He was still contending with censorship in certain quarters as well. In a letter to his friend Arthur Koestler he mentioned: "The French publisher who had signed a contract to translate *Animal Farm* has got cold feet and says it is impossible 'for political reasons.' It's really sad to think of a thing like that happening in France, of all countries in the world."

Orwell was upset by how his book was being misinterpreted. It was not a critique of all revolutions or all types of communism, he pointed out to those who would listen, but an indictment of the abuse of power. He still believed in socialism, but thought that if it was to be successful, it must avoid the tyrannical path taken by the Russian Revolution. Rather than give up on change entirely, he urged that people be suspicious of their leaders and that they empower themselves rather than rely on cult figures. Above all, he wanted to alert the public to situations where "All animals are equal but some are more equal than others."

Although Orwell's book was more successful than he could ever have hoped, he continued to live in much the same fashion as he always had. Thanks to his newfound popularity, work was more plentiful than ever, and in addition to his regular newspapers, he also began writing for the widely circulating *Evening Standard*. But he was still using work as a way to cope with Eileen's death. Soon, loneliness got the better of him, and he proposed marriage to at least two women in quick succession. He was as candid as ever about what he wanted: a mother for his child and someone to share his life and his literary estate. His proposals were honest but decidedly unromantic, and not even he was surprised when both women turned him down.

Now desperate for someone to help him care for his son, Orwell began to look for a housekeeper. He finally came across a young woman named Susan Watson. A divorcée who had a child of her own and also needed a source of income, Susan was eager to take the job. She got along well with Orwell, and he hired her shortly after their first meeting. He had a unique method for sizing her up, she later noted in a memoir. He took her out to dinner, excusing himself from the table just before the waiter arrived. After the waiter had left, Orwell emerged from a hiding place and informed her that he had ascertained her good character. The waiter had treated her well, and waiters, he claimed with authority, were the best judges of character.

Watson adapted quickly to Orwell's eccentric lifestyle. She learned that he took his tea incredibly strong, brewed with 11 spoonfuls, and ceased to be startled by his sometimes unusual requests. At one point, for instance, he suggested that she dye all his shirts blue, convinced that this would make his life much simpler. Initially surprised by how hard her new employer worked, Watson became so used to the sound of his typewriter during the night that she would wake with a start when it stopped. Orwell loved to work with tools as well, she later remembered, and instead of a teddy bear, Richard carried around his father's leather hammer, sleeping with it at night. Unceasingly generous, Orwell one day spontaneously gave all of Eileen's jewelry to Susan's daughter, Sally, after the little girl asked him what he was going to do with it.

Watson's help was indispensable to Orwell, for, workaholic though he was, his writing load was beginning to overwhelm him. Thanks to publicity from *Animal Farm,* he was besieged by requests for articles and conference appearances, and he began to turn them down with increasing frequency, not wanting the quality of his work to suffer. One of the essays he wrote at this time, "Politics and the English Language," argued that it was a writer's duty not to take shortcuts.

Like his essay on boys' weeklies, "Politics and the English Language" insisted on the significance of everyday phenomena. Something as ordinary as the arrangement of words in a sentence could have political implications: "The slovenliness of our language makes it easier for us to have foolish thoughts." It was an idea he was to develop even further in *Nineteen Eighty-four,* where Newspeak is used as a sinister way to curb individual freedom through language. Clear writing, Orwell argued, was particularly essential in a time when words like "elimination," used in World War II's Fascist regimes, functioned as euphemisms to condone the murder of millions.

Orwell finally thought of an appealing way out of his hectic lifestyle in London. David Astor had once mentioned to him that the island of Jura, off the coast of Scotland, would serve as a perfect retreat from city life. Orwell took the idea one step further. He loved the quiet of the country-side, and wished to see his son grow up in an outdoor environment. In 1946, on hearing that a farmhouse called Barnhill was available on a secluded part of the island, he decided to move there semi-permanently. The fact that the island had only about 300 people on it and was a 48-hour, two-boat journey from London added to its attraction for Orwell. Even the eight-mile hike to Barnhill from the main road—a long way for a sick man—did not give him pause.

Susan Watson joined Orwell and Richard on the island. In her memoir, she recalled the flurry of activity that preceded the move: "Our preparations involved an exciting shopping spree for paraffin lamps, candles, oilskins, Wellingtons, snake bite serum and army surplus blankets." Once on the island, Orwell assumed the role of landowner with great enthusiasm, planting trees and vegetables near the house and keeping chickens and a pig. One of his friends noted that he even experimented with smoking fish in the grate of his bedroom. Compared to Robinson Crusoe by more than one onlooker, Orwell was in his element. He invited numerous friends and family members to visit him, and overtaxed himself as usual by arranging long expeditions around the island's wild shores.

One of these outings took a decided turn for the worse. Orwell was on a fishing expedition in a small boat, along with Richard and the children of his older sister Marjorie. Suddenly the party was plunged into danger: Orwell had carelessly misjudged the tides and the boat lost its outboard motor in the violent pitching that ensued. Shortly afterward, the boat capsized entirely, and the ill-fated group saved themselves by swimming to a nearby rock island, Orwell with his young son in tow. Once safely out of the water, they were forced to summon help by waving a shirt on the end of a fishing rod. Eventually, a passing lobster boat, unable to dock on the rough coastline, threw them a rope which they were able to climb across to safety.

The one drawback of Jura was that it separated Orwell from his latest love interest. He had recently met a glamorous young woman named Sonia Brownell. Attracted to her forceful personality and stately beauty, he had proposed to her early on in their relationship. Known by some as "the Venus of Euston Road," Sonia was an assistant to Cyril Connolly at *Horizon* magazine, and a well-known figure in London's literary circles. Though flattered by Orwell's attentions, she was not ready to leave her busy life in London for the isolation of Jura. For the time being, their affair was put on hold.

In the winter of 1946, Orwell left Jura temporarily for the more hospitable climate of London. He resumed his "As I Please" column in *Tribune* and wrote, among other things, a criticism of American *Vogue,* which had recently been brought to his attention when it included a profile of him as a writer to watch for. There was a bad fuel shortage in London due to the postwar economic slump, and Orwell, in poor health as usual, suffered from the cold. In a letter to a friend in the United States, he described his desperate straits in grim detail: "What I do is to light the fires with a little of the coal I have left and keep them damped down all day with blocks of wet peat of which I happen to have a few." At one point, he was even forced to burn some of Richard's wooden toys to keep the house warm. He spent the winter looking forward to going back to his beloved island where, he told friends, the fuel situation was much better, for one could always forage for wood. He was eager to return for another reason, too: He was ready to start a new book that had been on his mind for some time.

In spring 1947, back on Jura, Orwell started working on the book that was to make him a legend. *Nineteen Eighty-four* was both a vision of the future and a collage of his past experiences. The futuristic novels he had read, such as *Brave New World* by his onetime teacher, Aldous Huxley, influenced him to some extent. But the world he created also drew on his persecution in Spain, his abhorrence of Stalin's Russia, his experience at the BBC, and the real-life gloom and squalor of postwar England. It was a nightmarish world ruled in Fascist form, with the will of the individual erased entirely by the repressive forces of the state. The grimness of *Nineteen Eighty-four's* vision was summed up by one of its characters, who said, "If you want a picture of the future, imagine a boot stamping on a human face—forever." Originally, Orwell was thinking of calling his new novel *The Last Man in Europe,* but nothing in the process of writing *Nineteen Eighty-four,* it turned out, went unrevised. Instead, the novel was a struggle for Orwell from start to finish. He was sick and getting sicker, but determined to produce another masterpiece. At the end of 1947, he had finished a first draft but thought it a "ghastly mess."

Orwell was himself in bad shape. He had managed to hold onto the dregs of his health until a draft was completed, but thereafter declined rapidly. Wrenching coughing episodes overcame him, and again he was coughing up blood. He was forced to leave Jura and check into Hairmyres Hospital on the Scottish mainland. There, doctors told him that he had advanced tuberculosis of the left lung. Forbidden to engage in any taxing activity, he was kept in the hospital for seven long months. Denied the use of his typewriter, he begged friends to keep him supplied with pens, and whiled away the hours doing journalistic writing and jotting down thoughts for a second draft of *Nineteen Eighty-four*. David Astor, anxious to help his gravely ill friend, arranged to have a new tuberculosis drug, strepto-mycin, sent over from the United States (antibiotics such as this one were still in the early stages of development and very hard to obtain). The treatment seemed to help. Despite numerous alarming side effects, such as the loss of patches of skin, Orwell finally felt stronger and healthier.

Soon, he was able to go home. Though he had been strongly advised against returning to Jura in his enfeebled condition, he made his way back there anyway, determined to finish his novel at any cost. He worked at it with a frantic intensity that distressed those around him. Not even his sister, Avril, who had taken over Susan Watson's role as Richard's caretaker, was able to slow him down. In November 1948, he finally declared the book finished.

The manuscript still needed to be typed, however, and Orwell wanted to supervise the task. He told his publisher, "I can't send it away because it is an unbelievably bad [manuscript] and no one could make head or tail of it without explanation." Needless to say, he was unable to get a typist to come to the island to perform the task. Doggedly, he determined to do the job himself and, using the last ounce of his strength, plugged away at his typewriter until it was done.

One month later, the manuscript was sent to Fredric Warburg in London. In the wake of Gollancz's rejection of *Animal Farm,* Orwell had asked to be released from his contract with his old publisher. Sensing that his new novel would be as important and controversial as the last, he wanted it to be published by the man who had always stood behind him: Warburg. Gollancz finally decided that it was only fair to let him go, and Warburg became his official publisher.

The work had left Orwell dangerously ill again, and this time he went to a sanatorium in Gloucestershire, far away from Jura. There, Warburg came to see him and congratulate him on his achievement. He had been so excited about the novel that he had written an appreciative report about it for his office colleagues. Together, Orwell and Warburg decided to call the novel *Nineteen Eighty-four*. It was published simultaneously in London and New York in June 1949, and was an instant success.

Nineteen Eighty-four is set in a hideously repressive, desolate future world where war is a constant fact of daily life, any form of creativity is suppressed, and gin lunches are served at government canteens to keep employees "happy." The story focuses on the demoralizing existence of a character named Winston Smith, who works for the government of Oceania—an immense superpower bloc—in the province of Airstrip One, formerly known as England. The government's inhumanity is summed up by the three Party slogans that justify its daily misdeeds, "War is Peace, Freedom is Slavery, Ignorance is Strength." Big Brother, the sinister Party leader, "watches" individuals from posters plastered on every available city wall and inspires fear and a slavish love in his subjects by holding "Two Minute Hates": political rallies in which his televised image stirs crowds into murderous frenzies directed at enemies abroad.

Winston's job for the Ministry of Truth is to support the Party by publishing lies that cover up the state's abusive methods. As well as the past, the state controls the present, by monitoring all individuals through two-way TV screens stationed in homes and workplaces. Any evidence of rebellion is followed up by a visit from the "Thought Police" and the eventual "elimination" of rebels. Despite the state's vigilant efforts at mind control, Winston, as he goes blankly through the mind-numbing routine of hate speeches and enforced exercise classes, begins to have rebellious thoughts

text continues on page 94

LETTER TO GWEN O'SHAUGHNESSY

After overexerting himself in his effort to finish Nineteen Eighty-four, *Orwell was in bad physical shape. In November 1948, he wrote to Gwen O'Shaughnessy, Eileen's sister-in-law, who was a doctor, to get a recommendation for a sanatorium where he would be able to rest and recuperate. The letter exhibits his understated attitude to his health, his affection for his son, and his determination to work on* Nineteen Eighty-four *himself, after his failure to procure a typist (the "stenog," a unique shorthand for stenographer, that he refers to at the end of the letter). It also, humorously, displays his negative attitude toward the pig he kept on Jura. He told a friend at one point that it was perhaps not surprising that the author of* Animal Farm *should not get along with a pig.*

Dear Gwen,

I wonder whether you know of a private sanatorium where they would be likely to have room for me. I have not felt really well since September, and sometimes felt very bad, and I thought it would be a good idea to go into a sanatorium for the worst of the winter, i.e. January and February and perhaps part of March. Dr. Dick agreed with me and recommended me to a place called the Grampian Sanatorium at Kingussie, which is the only private sanatorium in Scotland. However, they are full up. I have no doubt there are many more in England, however. It must be a private place, because the public ones will all have waiting lists, and also I must have a room to myself, otherwise I can't work. I can't of course pay things like 30 guineas a week, but can pay anything reasonable. Do you know of anywhere?

I hope the kids are well. All is well here and Richard is bursting with energy. He goes out fishing with the others now, and sometimes catches quite a lot of fish. The weather just lately has been very nice, beautiful still

At his secluded residence on the remote island of Jura off the rocky Scottish coast, Orwell wrote much of Nineteen Eighty-four.

sunny days and not at all cold, but I hardly ever go out of doors because the smallest exertion upsets me. The pig has grown to a stupendous size and goes to the butcher next week. We are all longing to get rid of him, as he is so destructive and greedy, even gets into the kitchen sometimes. Bill has got a young bull which seems quite a nice quiet beast and I trust will remain so. Avril is going up to London for a week or so in December to do some shopping and to see about giving up the Islington flat, which I don't want to keep on as it is simply an expense. I have finished my book, which I had been messing about with since some time in 1947. I am busy typing it out now, a ghastly job as it tires me to sit up much and I have to do most of it in a sofa. I tried to get a stenog to come here for a fortnight and do it for me, but the arrangements went wrong. Avril sends love. . . .

and looks for others to share his lonely vision of a better world. He finds a partner in Julia, a fellow civil servant, and together the two endeavor to find a way to oppose Big Brother and his oppressive regime. Their quest is ultimately doomed. The Party fiendishly second-guesses their actions and tortures them into confessions and mutual betrayal. Orwell's imagination had never been darker, nor more vivid, than it was in this final novel.

Orwell once said that *Nineteen Eighty-four* would have been a better book if he had not been so ill while writing it, but the public obviously did not agree with him. The *New York Times Book Review* called it "the most contemporary novel of this year," and renowned critics Lionel Trilling and V. S. Pritchett joined in the chorus of praise. Orwell's success as an author was sealed; the news of his fame spread rapidly and publishers around the world were soon clamoring for translations. The Book-of-the-Month Club, following up on its success with *Animal Farm,* was eager to make Orwell's latest novel one of its selections. But this time they wanted to edit the novel, cutting out the appendix Orwell had written on "The Principles of Newspeak" as well as "The Theory and Practice of Oligarchical Collectivism," a long document in the novel that denounces Big Brother's oppressive regime and inspires Winston Smith in his rebellion against the government. Despite the large sum of money at stake, Orwell refused to make the changes, feeling that they would alter the meaning of his book. Eventually, the book club agreed to publish it anyway, much to the writer's satisfaction.

With the success of *Nineteen Eighty-four,* Orwell was again the subject of controversy. Various critics accused him of undermining socialism and satirizing the newly elected British Labour Party. Warburg, in defense of Orwell, issued a press statement, bluntly stating that the book was not an attack on socialism. Orwell himself answered queries with equal frankness. In one letter, he wrote: "I do not believe that the kind of society I describe necessarily *will* arrive, but I believe (allowing of course for the fact that the book is a satire) that something resembling it could arrive.... Totalitarianism, if not fought against, could triumph anywhere." His novel, in other words, was not a prophecy but a warning.

In recent years, reports have surfaced that Orwell was so wary of the possibility of totalitarianism in England in the 1940s that he sent a list of possible communist sympathizers to the British Foreign Office, stating that those on the list "should not be trusted as propagandists." Clearly, *Nineteen Eighty-four* was his one-man effort at counterpropaganda.

His latest effort to inform the public of the perils of Fascism came at a heavy personal cost, however. The new drugs he had been given were no longer helping him, and his condition was rapidly getting worse. In the spring, his erstwhile romantic interest, Sonia Brownell, came back into his life. Impressed by the success of his latest novel and alarmed by news of his condition, she visited him in the sanatorium. Orwell now knew that his illness was probably fatal. But he felt that with someone at his side to care for him, he might have the strength to keep fighting it. He renewed his proposal to Sonia, and this time she accepted.

In need of a change of scene and more advanced treatment, Orwell was eventually moved to the University College Hospital in London. He was not unhappy to be back in London, for now, at least, he would be close to his new fiancée. Despite his relative good humor, friends who visited him were shocked by his haggard and emaciated appearance. He had become so thin that the doctors had difficulty finding a fleshy place on his body in which to give him injections. His friends T. R. Fyvel and journalist and political writer Malcolm Muggeridge, asked to discuss *Nineteen Eighty-four* on the radio, tried to be lighthearted in case Orwell was listening. They joked about how the novel's torture scene was reminiscent of the kind of torture small boys would devise at night in boarding school, before an

Alfresco at Ritz Representative
after the wedding of:
George Orwell & Sonia
Eric Blair   Mary Brownell

Robotke

MENU

Huitres

Filets de Sole d'Antin

Supreme de Volaille à la Ritz

Haricots Verts

Pommes Noisette

Poire Melba

Sonia Blair

Café

13th October 1949.

On his wedding day, Orwell was too sick to leave his hospital bed to attend the wedding dinner at the Ritz. A number of guests signed the menu card and presented it to him afterward as a memento.

adult yelled at them to turn out the lights. Their thoughtfulness paid off: Orwell apparently laughed out loud upon hearing the show.

In October 1949, Sonia and Orwell were married. Orwell was unable to leave the hospital, so the ceremony took place at his bedside, with David Astor as the best man. Uncharacteristically dapper for the day, Orwell wore a cherry-colored velvet smoking jacket. He was visibly cheerful, and the wedding was a happy occasion, for he now felt he might have the strength to fight his illness. He ardently wanted to live long enough to watch his son grow up. Sadly, his sickness had prevented him from seeing much of Richard, now 5; the boy was kept away from the hospital for fear he would catch his father's disease. Orwell got continual updates on his progress from Avril, however, and shared them with his friends in fatherly pride. Sentences like this one, from a note to his friend the novelist and literary critic Anthony Powell, were frequently featured in his letters: "Richard is offensively well & full of violence. He went through whooping cough without noticing that he had it." Orwell was so vigilant about his son's health that he even bought a tuberculosis-tested cow for Richard's milk, to minimize his possible exposure to the disease.

Despite his optimism about his potential for recovery, Orwell's strength was steadily slipping away. Though he made plans for the future, and once said hopefully that an author surely could not die while he still had works left to write, Malcolm Muggeridge, visiting him in December, saw little cause for hope. On returning from the hospital, Muggeridge wrote in his diary that "the stench of death was in the air, like autumn in the garden." Nonetheless, Orwell made ambitious plans to repair his health. He arranged to charter a plane to Switzerland where, it was thought, the clear mountain air might be beneficial to his damaged lungs. He did, however, take the precaution of drawing up a will before his journey, naming Avril the official guardian of his young son.

On January 21, 1950, with four days left before he was due to leave for Switzerland, Orwell suddenly suffered a massive hemorrhage of the lung. He died the same day, at the age of 46. Julian Symons, a friend and noted critic, wrote his obituary for *Tribune*. A touching tribute that reflected the admiration and respect he had inspired in many, the eulogy ended with the words: "He will be remembered as a writer particularly by *Animal Farm:* but he should be remembered equally as a man whose unorthodoxy was valuable in an age of power worship, who brought to the literature of our age the rare assets of a courageous spirit and a generous mind."

Orwell had stated that he wanted to be buried according to the rites of the Church of England. Though he had never been religious, his choice of a traditional burial showed that he remained patriotic, even at the end. A funeral service was announced at Christ Church and David Astor found a country churchyard in the Thames Valley, a region that Orwell had loved, in which to bury him. A rosebush was planted over his grave, in accordance with a wish he had once expressed. His gravestone was a simple one. On it were engraved the dates of his birth and death, along with the name by which his friends always knew him: Eric Blair.

Edmond O'Brien plays Winston Smith in this still from the 1956 film version of Nineteen Eighty-four.
The film's dramatic tagline read "Will Ecstasy Be a Crime . . . in the Terrifying World of the Future?"

ORWELL'S LEGACIES

Though George Orwell said, shortly before he died, that he still had more books to write, he had managed to achieve a formidable amount during his lifetime. He had written nine full-length books and an impressive 700 or so essays and articles. The success and appeal of his last two books sealed his fame internationally, and he would forever be compared to world-class writers such as Jonathan Swift and Voltaire. Over time, his name became a household word, and he is now one of the best-known English writers of the 20th century.

His books and essay collections have sold millions of copies around the world—*Nineteen Eighty-four* alone has sold more than 14 million English-language copies to date—and his work has been translated into as many as 60 languages. Though read and enjoyed by adults, *Animal Farm* and *Nineteen Eighty-four* are now also required reading in many schools and colleges, used to introduce students to the question of individual freedom in modern society. So widely read are these novels that they have become a cultural reference point, part of the common language we use to talk about politics and the role of government.

As evidence of this, our conversations and writings have become permeated with "Orwellisms." Words or phrases taken from Orwell's writing that have passed into the language can even be found in dictionaries and phrasebooks. "Orwellian" has become an adjective used to warn of anything that reeks of Fascism or repression. From *Animal Farm,* the slogan "all animals are equal but some are more equal than others" is regularly used as an ironic comment on unfair systems that pose as democratic ones, and from the totalitarian world of *Nineteen Eighty-four,* a range of words has been drawn to describe abuses of government and power. Politicians and the media are often accused of "Newspeak" and "doublethink." Those who censor themselves or others are called "Thought Police." The phrase "Big Brother" is also popular with people who wish to protest government interference in private life, such as the use of cameras to survey public areas like parks.

The degree to which Orwell's work has become part of our vocabulary was brought home in 1984, when a dramatic and unusually creative commercial flashed across viewers' screens during the Super Bowl intermission. It depicted a colorless world in which drab, weary men in uniform march through hallways lined with television screens. At the end of the hall, the men assemble in a stadium, transfixed by an enormous screen on which a "Big Brother" character feeds them propaganda, which they digest passively. Suddenly, a woman in bright-colored sports clothes comes running down the hall, pursued by uniformed guards.

The woman swings a ball and chain over her head, and before the guards can reach her, manages to launch it at the screen, smashing the icon to pieces. The spell has been broken: A triumphant message flashes across the screen hailing the arrival of Apple computers. Big Brother, it turned out, was meant to represent "Big Blue," the nickname of IBM, the company that then dominated the computer industry. The ad cast Apple in the role of the

lowly but resilient individual, determined to break free of the big company's monopolizing power. Its slogan informed viewers that when Apple computers arrived "You'll see why 1984 won't be like *Nineteen Eighty-four.*"

Though Orwell might not have liked his ideas being used as "propaganda" for an ad, the fact that such an expensive ad depended on its audience recognizing the reference to Orwell's book was proof indeed that the writer's work had become general knowledge. That year also saw the release of a film version of *Nineteen Eighty-four,* starring John Hurt and Richard Burton, with music by the Eurythmics. It was neither the first or last film to be made from one of his novels. The numerous adaptations of his novels into other genres—ranging from film and television to comic strips—bear witness to their enduring popularity.

Part of the reason for Orwell's lasting renown is that many of his concerns continue to be our own. Though the Soviet totalitarianism that fueled his imagination in *Animal*

The love of Winston (John Hurt) and Julia (Suzanna Hamilton) is doomed in Orwell's future world governed by Big Brother, shown here in Michael Radford's 1984 film adaptation of Nineteen Eighty-four.

Farm has become a thing of the past, the ongoing threat of war that plagued *Nineteen Eighty-four*'s characters is still with us, and his imaginary world of rival power blocs has more or less been realized. Some critics have pointed out that *Animal Farm*'s and *Nineteen Eighty-four*'s vision of the individual being inevitably crushed by the state has been belied by recent history, for groups of political dissidents around the world have had the strength to hold out against the most powerful state and imperial tyrannies. However, Orwell might respond that today's multinational corporations, with their own version of "propaganda"—advertising—and their ability to dictate the distribution of wealth around the world, carry on the threat to individual freedom that he had located in the state.

Although Orwell's fictional warnings and political writings bequeathed us a vocabulary with which to alert ourselves to various forms of repression, he also contributed to a more democratic society through his work at the BBC and his criticism of popular culture. At the BBC, his programming of university-level literary discussions paved the way for the kind of open university courses that now make education more widely accessible, and his perceptive analyses of everyday cultural artifacts, such as postcards and nonsense poetry, helped to undermine the prevalence of a class-based literary criticism.

Orwell had always been a contradictory figure. Accused of being both a snob and a revolutionary, he was at once nostalgic for the past and eager to change the world, an anti-intellectual who expanded the arena of intellectual topics. It is perhaps because of these contradictions that his persona and work have endured for so long and had the ability to appeal to so many. His willingness to engage with life and to live out his contradictions, regardless of the consequences, continues to inspire countless readers and writers to persevere in their own particular vision of political freedom.

CHRONOLOGY

1903
Eric Arthur Blair is born in Bengal, India, on June 25

1907
Moves to England with his mother and sister

1911–16
Attends St. Cyprian's

1917–21
Attends Eton

1922–27
Serves in imperial police force in Burma

1928–29
Lives in Paris; writes first professional articles for newspapers

1930
Returns to parents' house in Southwold, England

1931
Lives on and off as a tramp in the East End of London

1932
Teaches at The Hawthorns school

1933
Down and Out in Paris and London published under pen name
George Orwell

1934
Burmese Days published

1935
A Clergyman's Daughter published

1936
Marries Eileen O'Shaughnessy and moves to Wallington;
commissioned to write *The Road to Wigan Pier*

1937
Joins POUM militia in Spain; *The Road to Wigan Pier*
published

1938
Homage to Catalonia published; goes to Marrakech

1939
Returns from Marrakech; World War II starts; *Coming Up for Air* published

1940
Joins Home Guard in London

1941
Accepts position as Talks Assistant at the BBC

1943–45
Works as literary editor of *Tribune*

1944
Adopts a child, Richard Horatio Blair

1945
Goes to France as war correspondent; returns on hearing of Eileen's death; *Animal Farm* published

1946
Moves to Jura; begins work on *Nineteen Eighty-four*

1947–48
Hospitalized for tuberculosis; revises *Nineteen Eighty-four*

1949
Nineteen Eighty-four published; marries Sonia Brownell

1950
Dies of tuberculosis at University College Hospital, January 21; buried at All Saints Church in the village of Sutton Courtenay

FURTHER READING

MAJOR BOOKS BY GEORGE ORWELL

Down and Out in Paris and London. London: Gollancz, 1933. Reprint, New York: Harcourt Brace, 1983.

Burmese Days. London: Gollancz, 1934. Reprint, New York: Harcourt Brace, 1989.

A Clergyman's Daughter. London: Gollancz, 1935. Reprint, New York: Harcourt Brace, 1969.

Keep the Aspidistra Flying. London: Gollancz, 1936. Reprint, New York: Harcourt Brace, 1989.

The Road to Wigan Pier. London: Gollancz, 1937. Reprint, New York: Harcourt Brace, 1973.

Homage to Catalonia. London: Secker and Warburg, 1938. Reprint, New York: Harcourt Brace, 1987.

Coming Up for Air. London: Gollancz, 1939. Reprint, New York: Harcourt Brace, 1983.

Animal Farm. London: Secker and Warburg, 1945. Reprint, New York: Harcourt Brace, 1990.

Nineteen Eighty-four. London: Secker and Warburg, 1949. Reprint, New York: Harcourt Brace, 1983.

ORWELL'S ESSAYS AND OTHER WRITINGS

Orwell, Sonia and Ian Angus, eds. *Collected Essays, Journalism and Letters of George Orwell*. New York: Harcourt Brace, 1978.

West, W. J., ed. *The Lost Writings*. New York: Arbor House, 1985.

West, W. J., ed. *The War Commentaries*. London: Penguin, 1985.

BOOKS ABOUT ORWELL

Buddicom, Jacintha. *Eric and Us: A Remembrance of George Orwell*. London: Lewis Frewin, 1974.

Coppard, Audrey, and Bernard Crick, eds. *Orwell Remembered*. London: Ariel Books (BBC), 1984.

Crick, Bernard. *George Orwell: A Life*. London: Penguin, 1992.

Davison, Peter. *George Orwell: A Literary Life*. New York: St. Martin's Press, 1996.

Fyvel, T. R. *George Orwell*. New York: Macmillan, 1992.

Gross, Miriam, ed. *The World of George Orwell*. New York: Simon and Schuster, 1971.

Kalechofsky, Roberta. *George Orwell*. New York: Frederick Ungar, 1971.

Lewis, Peter. *George Orwell: The Road to "Nineteen Eighty-four."* New York: Harcourt Brace Jovanovich, 1981.

Shelden, Michael. *Orwell: The Authorized Biography*. New York: HarperCollins, 1991.

Smith, David, and Michael Mosher. *Orwell for Beginners*. New York: Writers and Readers Publishing Cooperative, 1984.

Thompson, John. *Orwell's London*. New York: Schocken, 1985.

Williams, Raymond. *Orwell*. London: Fontana, 1971.

FILM AND TV ADAPTATIONS OF ORWELL'S WORKS

Keep the Aspidistra Flying. Dir. Robert Bierman, 1997.

Nineteen Eighty-four. Dir. Michael Radford, 1984.

Coming Up for Air. Dir. Christopher Morahan, 1965. (Made for BBC television).

Nineteen Eighty-four. Dir. Christopher Morahan, 1965. (Made for BBC television).

Nineteen Eighty-four. Dir. Michael Anderson, 1956.

Animal Farm. Dir. Joy Batchelor and John Halas, 1955.

INDEX

ACKNOWLEDGMENTS

I wish to thank the Orwell Archive at University College, London, for allowing me access to their outstanding collection of materials on Orwell; Kristin Kiehn, Stephen Morrison, and Vanessa Manhire for their helpful input on various stages of the manuscript; Nancy Toff and Laura Brown for their encouragement and mentoring, and Karen Fein, for guiding me through the publication process. Finally, I am deeply grateful to my family and to Chris O'Brien for their unswerving support and inspiring work habits.

Picture Credits

Text Credits

Tanya Agathocleous is a Ph.D. candidate in Literatures in English at Rutgers University and has taught courses in British literature, world literature, and expository writing. Agathocleous is a contributor to the *Oxford Companion to United States History* and the *Cambridge Companion to George Eliot* and a coauthor of *Museum New York*. She holds a B.A. from Brown University.

22⁰⁰

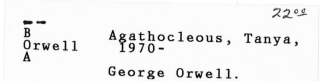

B
Orwell   Agathocleous, Tanya,
A   1970-

            George Orwell.

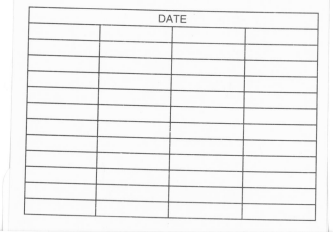

DATE			